OXFORD

Mastermaths 3

Paul Briten

3

Oxford University Press

Oxford University Press, Great Clarendon Street, Oxford OX2 6DP

Oxford New York

Athens Auckland Bangkok Bogota Bombay
Buenos Aires Calcutta Cape Town Dar es Salaam
Delhi Florence Hong Kong Istanbul Karachi
Kuala Lumpur Madras Madrid Melbourne
Mexico City Nairobi Paris Singapore
Taipei Tokyo Toronto Warsaw

and associated companies in
Berlin Ibadan

Oxford is a trade mark of Oxford University Press

© Paul Briten 1997

First published 1984
Reprinted 1985, 1989, 1991, 1993, 1994 (twice)
New Edition 1997

ISBN 0 19 834839 8

Typeset by Tradespools Ltd, Frome and Hardlines, Charlbury

Illustrated by CGS Studios, Cheltenham

Printed in Hong Kong

Contents

Contents

Assessment questions – key to levels:
black = level 3; orange = level 4; black in orange circle = level 5

A Name the shape in each picture:

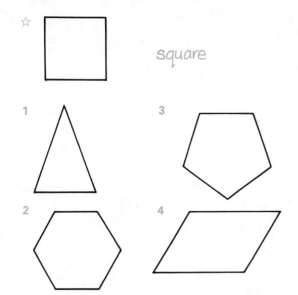

☆ square

1

2

3

4

B Name the shape of:

☆ a dice — cube

1 the magician's hat

4 this Egyptian tomb

2 the garden frame

5 the bean tin

3 this ice cream cornet

6 the box

C Use a mirror to work out each **symmetry message**:

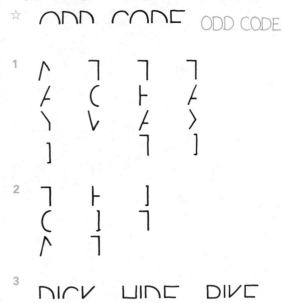

☆ ODD CODE

1

2

3

D You need a paper right angle. Are these angles right angles? Write **yes** or **no**:

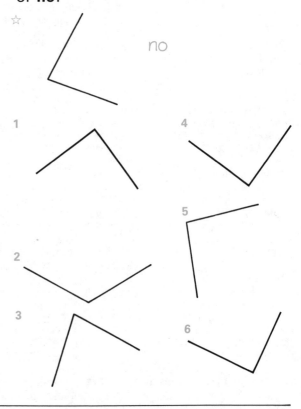

☆ no

1

4

2

5

3

6

Shape

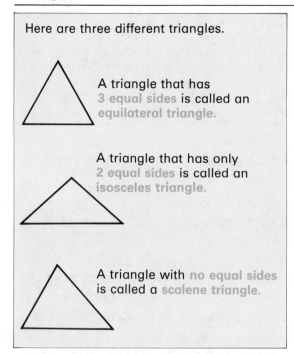

Here are three different triangles.

A triangle that has 3 equal sides is called an equilateral triangle.

A triangle that has only 2 equal sides is called an isosceles triangle.

A triangle with no equal sides is called a scalene triangle.

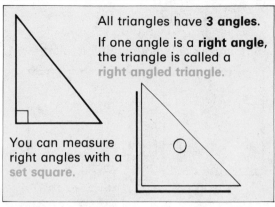

All triangles have **3 angles**.
If one angle is a **right angle**, the triangle is called a right angled triangle.

You can measure right angles with a set square.

A Measure the sides of these triangles. Write **equilateral, isosceles** or **scalene** for each one:

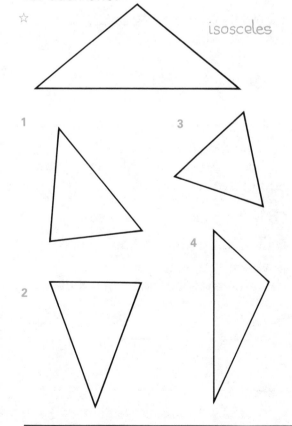

☆ isosceles

1

2

3

4

B Use a set square.
Are these triangles **right angled** triangles? Write **yes** or **no**:

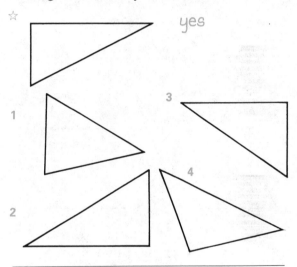

☆ yes

1

2

3

4

C Which triangles below are:

☆ right angled?   a and b

1 equilateral?

2 scalene?

3 isosceles?

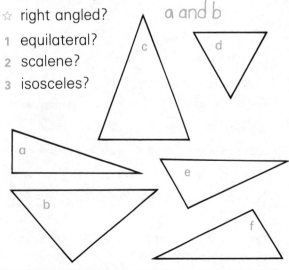

a

b

c

d

e

f

6 **Shape**

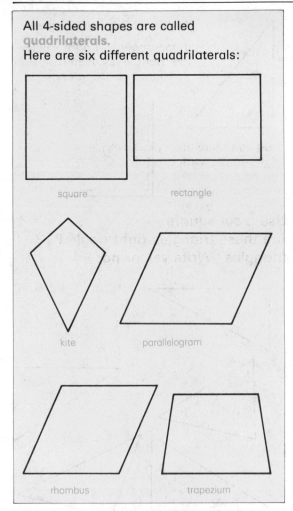

All 4-sided shapes are called
quadrilaterals.
Here are six different quadrilaterals:

square   rectangle

kite   parallelogram

rhombus   trapezium

A Which shapes above have:

☆ 4 right angles?

square, rectangle

1 no right angles?

2 4 sides equal in length?

3 opposite sides equal in length?

4 both pairs of opposite sides parallel?

5 no parallel sides?

6 4 equal sides and 4 right angles?

7 4 equal sides and no right angles?

8 both pairs of opposite sides parallel
and 4 right angles?

9 both pairs of opposite sides parallel
and no right angles?

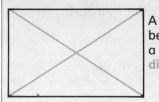

A straight line
between 2 corners in
a shape is called a
diagonal.

B 1 Copy this
square on
squared paper.

2 Draw 2
diagonals in
the square.

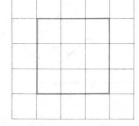

3 Are the angles where the diagonals
cross, greater than right angles, less
than right angles or right angles?

4 Your square is divided into 4
triangles. Are the triangles isosceles,
equilateral or scalene?

C 1 Copy this
rectangle on
squared paper.

2 Draw 2
diagonals in
the rectangle.

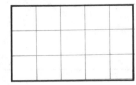

3 Your rectangle is divided into 4
triangles. Are the triangles **isosceles**,
equilateral or **scalene**?

D 1 Copy the shapes on squared paper.

2 Draw 2 **diagonals** in each shape.

3 In which shape are the angles
between the diagonals right angles?

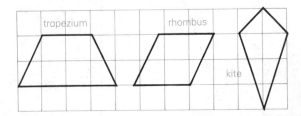

Shape

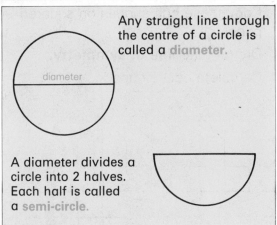

Any straight line through the centre of a circle is called a **diameter**.

A diameter divides a circle into 2 halves. Each half is called a **semi-circle**.

The edge of a circle is called the **circumference**.

The distance from the centre of a circle to the circumference is called the **radius**.

A Measure the **diameter** of each circle below, to the nearest centimetre:

2 cm

1

3

2

B Has each circle been divided into 2 semi-circles ? Write **yes** or **no**:

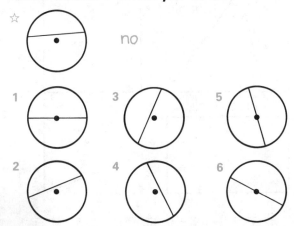

no

1

2

3

4

5

6

C Measure the **radius** of each circle below, to the nearest half centimetre:

1 cm

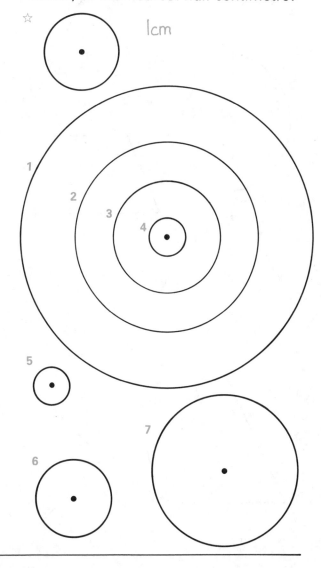

1

2

3

4

5

6

7

A Place a mirror along each dotted line. Write the name of each shape that you see:

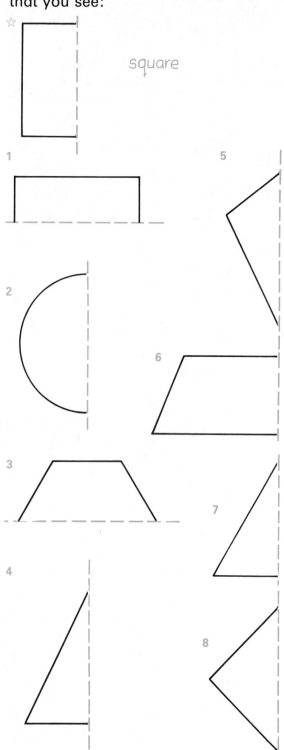

☆ square

1

2

3

4

5

6

7

8

B 1 Copy these half shapes on squared paper.

2 Draw in the **line of symmetry.**

3 Complete each shape.

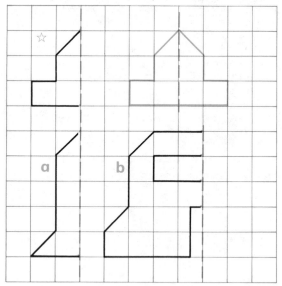

☆

a

b

C You need a mirror.
How many **lines of symmetry** has:

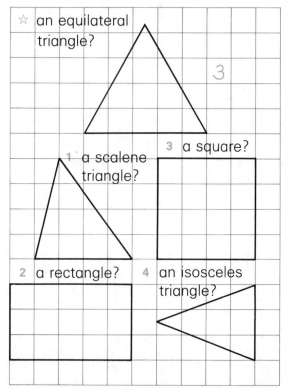

☆ an equilateral triangle?

3

1 a scalene triangle?

3 a square?

2 a rectangle?

4 an isosceles triangle?

A You need a sheet of squared paper and a partner.

Draw a line of symmetry down the centre of the paper.

Mark a point near the top of the line of symmetry.

Slowly draw one half of a symmetrical shape on the left of the line of symmetry. As you do this, your partner tries to draw the other half of the shape on the right of the line of symmetry.

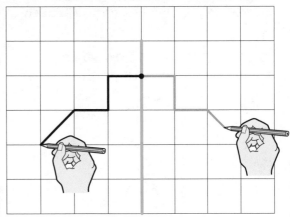

In the diagram you can see that if you draw a line one square to the left your partner must draw a line one square to the right.

Taking turns to draw first, try to draw in this way:

a) a robot   b) a house   c) a rocket

Try to draw some pictures in this way using plain paper.

B On thin card draw a square with sides of 12 cm.

Divide the square as shown in this diagram.

Cut out the pieces.

Can you rearrange the pieces to form:

a) a rectangle?   b) a parallelogram?

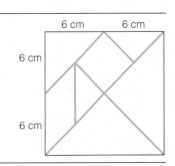

C You need some dotted paper.

On your paper draw 10 squares each of which has 16 dots inside.

In one of these squares join dots to make a parallelogram.

Using your other squares try to join dots to form
a) a square   b) an isosceles triangle
c) a scalene triangle   d) a trapezium
e) an equilateral triangle   f) a rectangle   g) a hexagon
h) a kite   i) a rhombus

Make a list of the shapes that you were able to draw and another list of those that you could not do.

Answer any questions you can. Leave those you cannot do.

For each triangle below write
isosceles, scalene **or** equilateral.

1

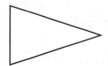

2

3

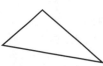

Measure the radius of each of these circles:

4

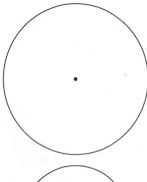

5

How many lines of symmetry has each of these shapes?

6

7

Name each of these shapes:

8

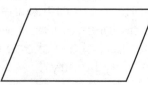

9

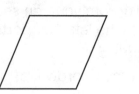

10

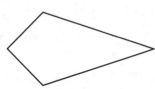

Each of these squares has been reflected in a mirror.

Which is the correct reflection, A, B or C?

11

12

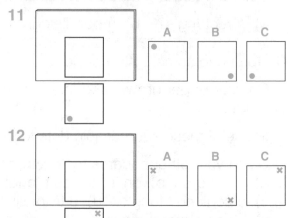

Angles

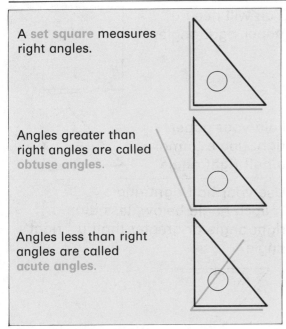

A **set square** measures right angles.

Angles greater than right angles are called **obtuse angles**.

Angles less than right angles are called **acute angles**.

A You need a set square.
Is each angle below an **acute angle**, an **obtuse angle** or a **right angle**?

☆

obtuse angle

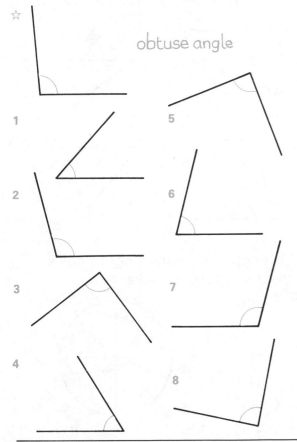

1

2

3

4

5

6

7

8

B Name each of the shapes below:

☆ a is a square

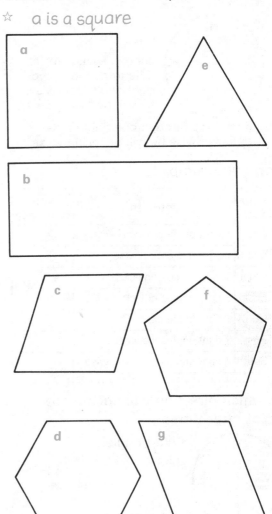

a

e

b

c

f

d

g

C Copy and complete this table for the shapes above:

shape	number of angles that are		
	acute	obtuse	right angles
☆ square	0	0	4
1			
2			
3			
4			
5			
6			

10 **Angles**

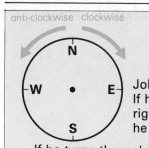

John is facing North. If he turns through one right angle clockwise, he will be facing East.

If he turns through one right angle anti-clockwise he will be facing west.

A Copy and complete:

you face	you turn	you now face
☆ East	1 right angle anti-clockwise	North
1 South	1 right angle clockwise	
2 West	2 right angles anti-clockwise	
3 East	3 right angles anti-clockwise	
4 North	1 right angle clockwise	
5 East	3 right angles clockwise	
6 South	2 right angles anti-clockwise	

B In which direction will each arrow point after turning:

☆ 3 right angles clockwise? East

1 2 right angles anti-clockwise?
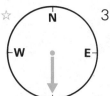

2 1 right angle clockwise?
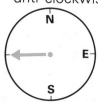

3 3 right angles anti-clockwise?
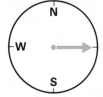

4 2 right angles clockwise?
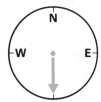

C You will need a paper right angle.
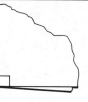

Fold your paper right angle to make a half right angle.

D Use your half right angle. Is each angle below, less than a $\frac{1}{2}$ right angle or greater than a $\frac{1}{2}$ right angle?

☆ greater

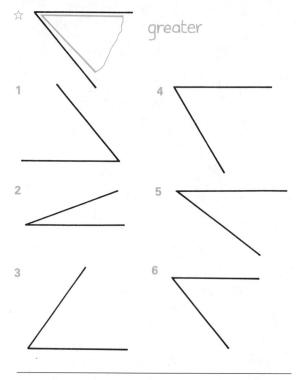

E Through how many $\frac{1}{2}$ right angles must you turn to make:

☆ $\frac{1}{4}$ turn? 2

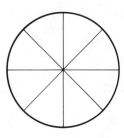

1 a full turn?
2 $\frac{1}{2}$ turn?
3 $\frac{3}{4}$ turn?

Angles

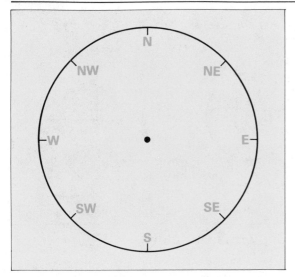

C Copy and complete:

	you face	you turn	you now face
☆	E	1½ right angles anti-clockwise	NW
1	S	1 right angle clockwise	
2	N	1½ right angles clockwise	
3	W	2 right angles anti-clockwise	
4	NE	2 right angles clockwise	
5	SW	2½ right angles anti-clockwise	
6	NW	3 right angles anti-clockwise	
7	SE	4 right angles anti-clockwise	
8	S	3½ right angles clockwise	

A Write out the **compass points** in full:

☆ NE   North-East

1	N	5	SE
2	W	6	SW
3	S	7	NW
4	E		

B In which direction is each ship sailing?

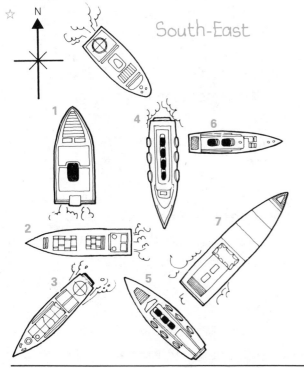

☆ South-East

D Through how many **right angles** must the telescope turn clockwise?

	pointing	turns to point	clockwise turn
☆	NE	S	1½ right angles
1	N	NE	
2	S	NW	
3	W	N	
4	E	SW	
5	NE	W	
6	NW	S	
7	SE	S	
8	SW	S	

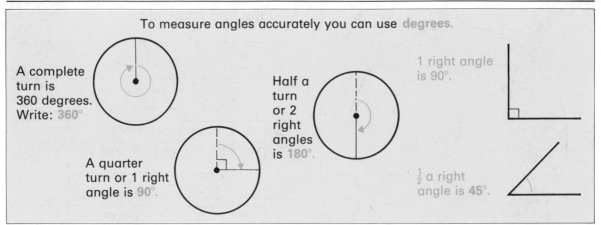

To measure angles accurately you can use degrees.

A complete turn is 360 degrees. Write: 360°

A quarter turn or 1 right angle is 90°.

Half a turn or 2 right angles is 180°.

1 right angle is 90°.

½ a right angle is 45°.

A Copy and complete:

turn	number of right angles	number of degrees
☆ 1 full turn	4	360°
1 ½ turn		
2 ¼ turn		
3 ¾ turn		

B Write these compass angles in **degrees**:

☆

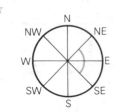

90°

1

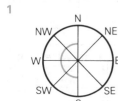

3

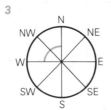

2

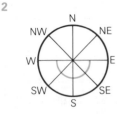

4

C Copy and complete:

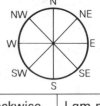

	I am facing	I turn clockwise through	I am now facing
☆	S	90°	W
1	N	180°	
2	E	90°	
3	W	45°	
4	SE	45°	
5	SW	135°	

D Are these angles **acute** angles or **obtuse** angles?

☆ 100° (larger than a right angle) obtuse

1 70°   5 68°

2 50°   6 95°

3 120°   7 36°

4 179°   8 86°

E Write **true** or **false**:

☆ 1 right angle > 50°   true

1 1 complete turn < 300°

2 ½ turn > 200°

3 ¼ turn = 90°

4 2 right angles = 200°

5 ½ right angle = 45°

Angle tangle

Follow this secret code to find the hidden message.
Write letters for ✳'s:

From Q, turn 2 right angles clockwise to U, *then*
turn 45° anti-clockwise to A, *then*
turn 90° clockwise to ✳, *then*
turn ½ right angle clockwise to ✳, *then*
turn 180° clockwise to ✳, *then*
turn 1½ right angles clockwise to ✳.
The first word is QUA————.

From T, turn 45° anti-clockwise to ✳, *then*
turn 90° anti-clockwise to ✳, *then*
turn 2½ right angles clockwise to ✳, *then*
turn ½ right angle clockwise to ✳.

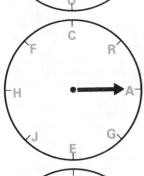

From A, turn ½ right angle anti-clockwise to ✳, *then*
turn 1½ right angles clockwise to ✳.

From R, turn ½ right angle anti-clockwise to ✳, *then*
turn 1½ right angles clockwise to ✳, *then*
turn 90° clockwise to ✳, *then*
turn ½ right angle anti-clockwise to ✳.

From A, turn 2 right angles anti-clockwise to ✳, *then*
turn 45° clockwise to ✳, *then*
turn 1½ right angles anti-clockwise to ✳, *then*
turn 45° anti-clockwise to ✳, *then*
turn 1 right angle clockwise to ✳.

A Write **equilateral, isosceles** or **scalene** for each of these triangles:

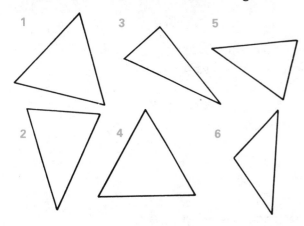

B What is the length of the **radius** and the **diameter** in each of these circles?

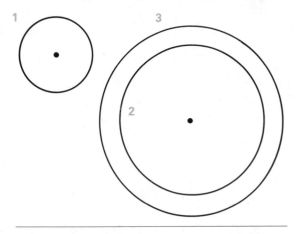

C How many **lines of symmetry** has:

1 a rectangle? 3 an equilateral triangle?

2 a kite? 4 a square?

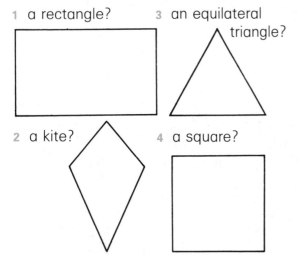

D Write **acute** or **obtuse** for each angle below:

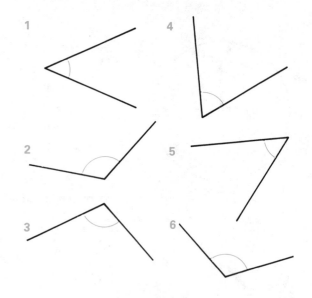

E Copy and complete:

	you face	you turn	you now face
☆	West	1½ right angles anti-clockwise	South-East
1	North	3 right angles clockwise	
2	East	1½ right angles clockwise	
3	North-West	½ right angle anti-clockwise	
4	South-West	2 right angles clockwise	
5	South	2½ right angles anti-clockwise	

F Write these compass angles in **degrees:**

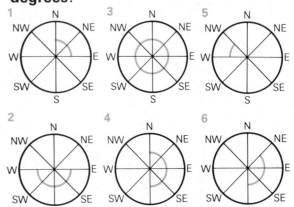

A Sam has written his name using moves and turns.

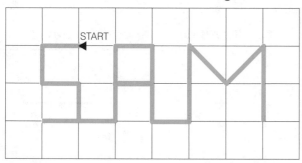

START

move forward	turn
1cm	1 right angle anti-clockwise
1cm	1 right angle anti-clockwise
1cm	1 right angle clockwise
1cm	1 right angle clockwise
1cm	2 right angles clockwise
2cm	

Copy and complete the table for Sam.

Make a table of moves and turns to spell out your name.

B A car follows these instructions to travel from A to B.

Forward 10, left 90°, forward 40, right 90°, forward 20.

Write a set of instructions for the car to travel from
a) A to C   b) A to D to E to F   c) A to C to D to F

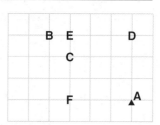

Using a Logo program on a computer, work out a set of instructions to draw:

a) a square   b) a rectangle   c) a parallelogram

C Copy and complete this table to lead the fly from point A to point C.

at point	fly facing	fly turns	walks forward	arrives at point
A	South	180° anti-clockwise	2cm	L
L	North	90° clockwise	1cm	S
S	East	45° clockwise		

Draw another table of instructions which leads the fly from L to G.

An injured fly with a broken leg can turn only anti-clockwise. Work out a set of instructions for this fly to travel from R to K.

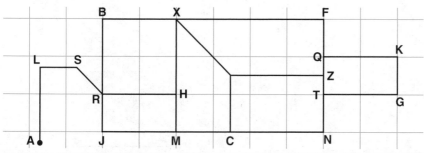

Answer any questions you can. Leave those you cannot do.

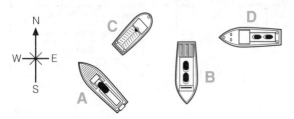

Which direction will be followed if:

1 ship A turns 3 right angles clockwise?

2 ship B turns 1½ right angles anti-clockwise?

3 ship C turns 2½ right angles clockwise?

4 ship D turns 3½ right angles anti-clockwise?

How many right angles in:

5 a square?

6 a rectangle?

7 a right-angled triangle?

8 a rhombus?

How many degrees in:

9 a quarter turn?

10 a full turn?

11 a half turn?

Write acute or obtuse for each of these angles:

12

13

14

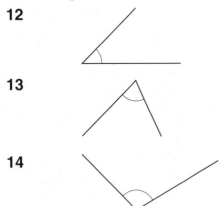

Copy and complete this table:

	I am facing	I turn anti-clockwise through	I am now facing
15	North	90°	
16	South		West
17	South-East	180°	
18		45°	North-West
19		135°	South-West

Write acute or obtuse for each of these angles:

20 82°

21 111°

22 98°

23 89°

Write true or false for each of the following:

24 You can draw a quadrilateral with 2 obtuse angles.

25 You can draw a triangle with 2 right angles.

26 You can draw a parallelogram with 3 acute angles.

Use a protractor to measure these angles:

27

28

Invaders

You need 25 counters.
Place a counter on the circle with the correct answer to each question below.

How many rockets reach their targets?

☆ 9+7= ✱ 16   5 8+9= ✱   10 6+12= ✱   15 12+9= ✱   20 6+7= ✱

1 16+8= ✱   6 23+8= ✱   11 9+17= ✱   16 8+7= ✱   21 19+9= ✱

2 30+14= ✱   7 19+16= ✱   12 14+18= ✱   17 16+20= ✱   22 15+15= ✱

3 18+7= ✱   8 24+9= ✱   13 10+12= ✱   18 19+19= ✱   23 8+11= ✱

4 14+13= ✱   9 50+27= ✱   14 7+7= ✱   19 21+19= ✱   24 16+13= ✱

   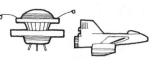

60	27	37	30	24	39
53	17	34	44	26	23
41	33	29	18	15	11
20	32	31	25	14	22
12	16	77	13	35	21
37	36	19	38	40	28

 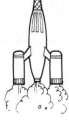     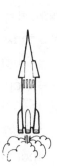

KEEP
OUT
ROCKET
FIRING

A Pencils are packed in **tens**.

How many full boxes and how many pencils left with:

☆ 94 pencils?   9 boxes 4 pencils left

1 62 pencils?
2 55 pencils?
3 82 pencils?
4 21 pencils?
5 17 pencils?
6 69 pencils?
7 96 pencils?
8 18 pencils?
9 20 pencils?
10 90 pencils?

B Rubbers are packed in **hundreds**.

How many boxes and how many rubbers left with:

☆ 462 rubbers?   4 boxes 62 rubbers left

1 325 rubbers?
2 168 rubbers?
3 273 rubbers?
4 456 rubbers?
5 824 rubbers?
6 690 rubbers?
7 300 rubbers?
8 207 rubbers?
9 311 rubbers?
10 806 rubbers?

C Write the number that is:

☆ 10 more than 165   175

1 10 more than 182
2 10 less than 463
3 100 more than 227
4 100 less than 965
5 1000 less than 4931
6 20 more than 666
7 50 less than 141
8 30 more than 82
9 30 less than 111
10 50 more than 96

D Write in figures:

☆ Two thousand three hundred and sixty-two   2362

1 Four hundred and nineteen
2 One thousand two hundred and ninety-four
3 Two thousand six hundred and twenty
4 Eight thousand and thirty-five
5 Seven thousand nine hundred
6 Three thousand and one
7 Five thousand five hundred
8 One thousand and ninety-one

E Write in thousands, hundreds, tens and units:

☆ 4356   4 thousands 3 hundreds 5 tens 6 units

1 2713
2 4568
3 3210
4 4762
5 1059
6 6604
7 3200
8 9000

F Write the sign < or > for ✳'s:

☆ 2651 ✳ 1256   >

1 1234 ✳ 4321
2 4226 ✳ 4662
3 1758 ✳ 1857
4 2371 ✳ 2317
5 6200 ✳ 6199
6 2411 ✳ 1249
7 3726 ✳ 3800
8 2001 ✳ 1999

G Write the value of each orange number:

☆ 3**2**7   20

1 4**1**6
2 **3**25
3 5**2**8
4 1**0**7
5 **8**06
6 **9**00
7 5**2**3
8 1**4**26
9 20**3**7
10 1**9**7
11 **8**632
12 **9**419
13 3**2**5
14 9106
15 197**0**

Addition

Add together 49, 27 and 15:

7 tens   21 units

change 20 units to 2 tens:
9 tens 1 unit

```
  49
  27
 +15
 ---
  91
   2
```

Add together 183, 264 and 187:

4 hundreds 22 tens 14 units

change 10 units to 1 ten:
4 hundreds 23 tens 4 units

change 20 tens to 2 hundreds:
6 hundreds 3 tens 4 units

```
  183
  264
 +187
 ----
  634
   2 1
```

A Copy and complete:

☆
```
  37        37
  14        14
 +29       +29
 ---       ---
            80
```

1
```
  25
  17
 +19
```

5
```
  26
  38
 +16
```

9
```
  15
  39
 + 7
```

2
```
  36
  18
 +27
```

6
```
  68
   9
 +17
```

10
```
  58
  17
 + 9
```

3
```
  49
  28
 +15
```

7
```
  26
  36
 +19
```

11
```
  42
  19
 +29
```

4
```
  15
  17
 +48
```

8
```
  17
  47
 +29
```

12
```
  28
  26
 +26
```

B Copy and complete:

☆
```
  245        245
  389        389
 +190       +190
 ----       ----
             824
```

1
```
  396
  184
 +253
```

5
```
  476
  152
 +183
```

9
```
  527
   99
 + 91
```

2
```
  265
  357
 +192
```

6
```
  137
  289
 +375
```

10
```
  247
  195
 +283
```

3
```
  176
  273
 +370
```

7
```
  274
  287
 +251
```

11
```
  183
  196
 +171
```

4
```
  224
   94
 +596
```

8
```
  566
  191
 +263
```

12
```
  248
  386
 +282
```

A Copy and complete:

☆
```
   279        279
   146        146
 +215       +215
 ____        640
             1 2
```

1
```
    27
    32
 +  19
```

3
```
   147
   329
 +139
```

5
```
   466
   194
 +183
```

2
```
   352
   173
 +  87
```

4
```
    48
    96
 +143
```

6
```
   379
   147
 +318
```

Add together 1237 and 1152:

2 thousands 3 hundreds 8 tens 9 units

```
  1237
 +1152
  2389
```

B Answer these questions:

☆ A sparrow makes 269 hops, 426 more hops and then another 58 hops. How many hops does it make altogether?

```
  269
  426
 + 58
  753
```

1 Mr Patel buys a fridge for £167, a colour television for £289 and a toaster for £15. What is the total cost of all 3 items?

2 Alice has 126 stamps, Jack has 387 stamps and Mike has 92 stamps. How many stamps do they have altogether?

3 In 3 throws of darts, Alex scores 125, 99 and 17. What is his total score?

4 John swims 163 metres, 179 metres and then another 496 metres. How far does he swim altogether?

C Copy and complete:

☆
```
 Th H T U      Th H T U
  6 4 1 2       6 4 1 2
 +1 3 8 7      +1 3 8 7
 _____       7 7 9 9
```

1
```
 Th H T U
  3 4 5 6
 +1 2 4 2
```

6
```
 Th H T U
  4 5 1 3
 +1 4 5 6
```

2
```
 Th H T U
  2 1 0 5
 +4 8 7 2
```

7
```
 Th H T U
  2 5 1 6
 +3 2 7 3
```

3
```
 Th H T U
  5 5 2 6
 +2 3 6 0
```

8
```
 Th H T U
  1 9 2 6
 +4 0 6 2
```

4
```
 Th H T U
  6 2 1 4
 +1 5 8 5
```

9
```
 Th H T U
  4 2 5 3
 +3 5 4 6
```

5
```
 Th H T U
  3 2 9 6
 +1 7 0 3
```

10
```
 Th H T U
  2 4 6 8
 +1 4 3 1
```

Addition

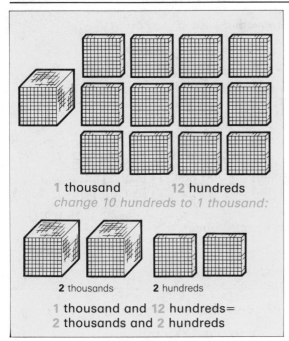

1 thousand 12 hundreds
change 10 hundreds to 1 thousand:

2 thousands   2 hundreds

1 thousand and 12 hundreds=
2 thousands and 2 hundreds

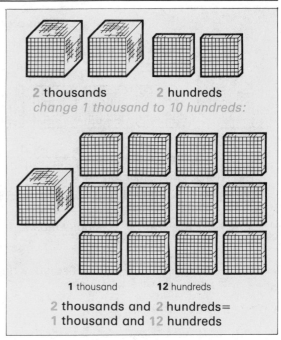

2 thousands   2 hundreds
change 1 thousand to 10 hundreds:

1 thousand 12 hundreds

2 thousands and 2 hundreds=
1 thousand and 12 hundreds

A Use apparatus if you need to.
Change **10** hundreds to **1** thousand.
Write numbers for ✻'s:

☆
1 thousand 13 hundreds=
✻ thousands ✻ hundreds

2 thousands 3 hundreds

1 2 thousands 11 hundreds=
✻ thousands ✻ hundreds

2 1 thousand 10 hundreds=
✻ thousands ✻ hundreds

3 1 thousand 14 hundreds=
✻ thousands ✻ hundreds

4 0 thousands 16 hundreds=
✻ thousand ✻ hundreds

5 2 thousands 15 hundreds=
✻ thousands ✻ hundreds

6 3 thousands 12 hundreds=
✻ thousands ✻ hundreds

7 4 thousands 13 hundreds=
✻ thousands ✻ hundreds

8 3 thousands 19 hundreds=
✻ thousands ✻ hundreds

B Use apparatus if you need to.
Change **1** thousand to **10** hundreds.
Write numbers for ✻'s:

☆ 3 thousands 4 hundreds=
✻ thousands ✻ hundreds

2 thousands 14 hundreds

1 2 thousands 4 hundreds=
✻ thousands ✻ hundreds

2 4 thousands 2 hundreds=
✻ thousands ✻ hundreds

3 3 thousands 1 hundred=
✻ thousands ✻ hundreds

4 5 thousands 9 hundreds=
✻ thousands ✻ hundreds

5 1 thousand 6 hundreds=
✻ thousands ✻ hundreds

C How many hundreds are there in:

☆ 2600? *26 hundreds*

1 1700?   4 2800?   7 4500?

2 1300?   5 1900?   8 2000?

3 2100?   6 3200?   9 6000?

10 hundreds = 1 thousand

Add together 1364 and 1822:

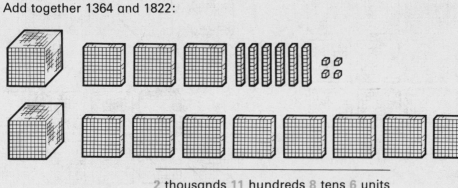

2 thousands 11 hundreds 8 tens 6 units

change 10 hundreds to 1 thousand:

3 thousands 1 hundred 8 tens 6 units

```
Th H T U
   1 3 6 4
 + 1 8 2 2
   3 1 8 6
       1
```

A Copy and complete:

```
☆  Th H T U        Th H T U
   2 7 1 5          2 7 1 5
 + 3 6 2 4        + 3 6 2 4
                    6 3 3 9
```

```
1  Th H T U      3  Th H T U
   1 7 9 4          6 6 2 0
 + 4 8 0 5        + 1 8 0 8
```

```
2  Th H T U      4  Th H T U
   6 3 5 7          8 1 7 4
 + 2 9 1 2        +   9 2 4
```

B Copy and complete:

```
☆    4 7 2 3        4 7 2 3
   + 1 0 9 4      + 1 0 9 4
                    5 8 1 7
```

```
1    2 4 6 8      4    3 8 5 2
   + 1 3 1 9        + 1 0 5 4
```

```
2    6 2 1 5      5    3 1 2 5
   + 1 3 9 1        + 4 1 0 8
```

```
3    3 4 5 2      6    2 4 1 9
   + 2 6 1 7        + 3 8 8 0
```

C Answer these questions:

☆ There are 1279 bees in one hive and 3910 bees in another hive. How many bees altogether?

```
   1 2 7 9
 + 3 9 1 0
   5 1 8 9
```

1 2643 cars were made in a factory in one year and 2426 cars in the next year. How many cars were made in the two years?

2 1627 books are sold at a bookshop in January and 1335 books in February. How many books were sold in the 2 months?

3 A group of 2527 ants meet another group of 3192 ants. How many ants are there altogether?

Addition

Add together 4248 and 3675:

```
  4 2 4 8
+ 3 6 7 5
  7 9 2 3
    1 1
```

Add together 3572 and 5836:

```
  3 5 7 2
+ 5 8 3 6
  9 4 0 8
    1 1
```

Add together 2743 and 3897:

```
  2 7 4 3
+ 3 8 9 7
  6 6 4 0
    1 1 1
```

A Copy and complete:

☆
```
  2 7 3 8        2 7 3 8
+ 3 4 2 4      + 3 4 2 4
                 6 1 6 2
```

1
```
  3 4 1 7
+ 2 9 0 6
```

5
```
  4 1 6 3
+ 3 6 4 7
```

2
```
  2 1 5 6
+ 3 2 6 5
```

6
```
  2 9 5 8
+ 3 7 0 9
```

3
```
  3 9 6 4
+ 1 3 2 7
```

7
```
  3 6 4 3
+ 2 5 7 6
```

4
```
  6 6 2 7
+ 1 5 8 2
```

8
```
  1 8 2 2
+ 5 4 8 9
```

B This table shows the money taken in a two week sale. Work out the total takings for each shop:

	week 1	week 2
☆ Blogg's	£3215	£2695
1 Boodle's	£4613	£2428
2 Nunn's	£2971	£3029
3 Harold's	£4667	£3296
4 Jason's	£3129	£2907
5 Will's	£7263	£5388

```
  £ 3 2 1 5
+ £ 2 6 9 5
  £ 5 9 1 0
```

C Copy and complete:

☆
```
  2 6 3 7        2 6 3 7
+ 1 4 8 5      + 1 4 8 5
                 4 1 2 2
```

1
```
  4 2 6 8
+ 3 9 6 2
```

4
```
  2 7 7 7
+ 1 6 6 7
```

2
```
  5 1 7 6
+ 2 8 7 4
```

5
```
  5 9 2 6
+ 3 8 8 8
```

3
```
  3 9 6 2
+ 4 8 7 9
```

6
```
  3 9 1 5
+ 2 0 8 6
```

D This table shows the amount of drinks sold at a pop concert:

lemonade	1758 litres
coke	2465 litres
orange	879 litres
blackcurrant	1657 litres
bitter lemon	966 litres

What were the total sales of:

☆ lemonade and orange?

```
  1 7 5 8 l
+   8 7 9 l
  2 6 3 7 l
```

1 coke and blackcurrant?

2 bitter lemon and lemonade?

3 coke and orange?

4 orange and blackcurrant?

Follow the correct answers. Write down the letters on each object you reach.
Work out the 'Message to sailors'.

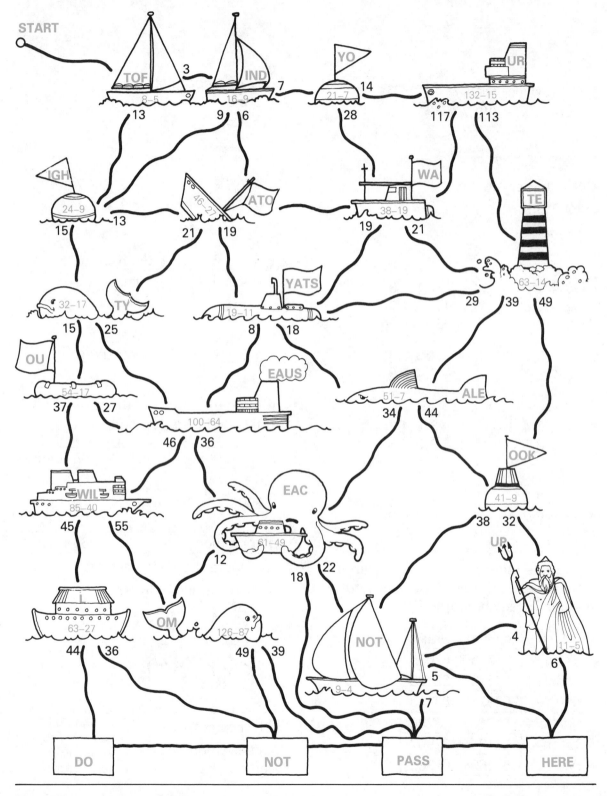

Subtraction

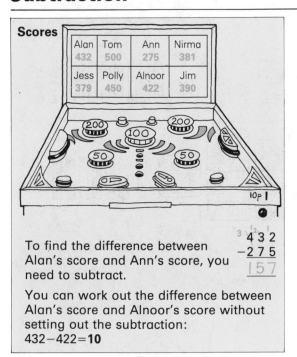

Scores

Alan	Tom	Ann	Nirma
432	500	275	381
Jess	Polly	Alnoor	Jim
379	450	422	390

To find the difference between Alan's score and Ann's score, you need to subtract.

$$\begin{array}{r} {}^3\cancel{4}{}^{12}\cancel{3}{}^1 2 \\ -\ 2\ 7\ 5 \\ \hline 1\ 5\ 7 \end{array}$$

You can work out the difference between Alan's score and Alnoor's score without setting out the subtraction:
432−422=**10**

From 2437 subtract 1225:

subtract 1 2 2 5:

1 thousand **2** hundreds **1** ten and **2** units are left.

$$\begin{array}{r} Th\ H\ T\ U \\ 2\ 4\ 3\ 7 \\ -\ 1\ 2\ 2\ 5 \\ \hline 1\ 2\ 1\ 2 \end{array}$$

A Set out the subtraction only if you need to.

What is the **difference** in score between:

☆ Jess and Nirma?

    2

1 Nirma and Jim?

2 Jess and Jim?

3 Alan and Polly?

4 Polly and Tom?

5 Tom and Jim?

6 Jim and Ann?

7 Jess and Polly?

8 Ann and Tom?

9 Jim and Polly?

10 Tom and Alan?

11 Polly and Alnoor?

12 Nirma and Polly?

B Copy and complete:

☆
$$\begin{array}{r} Th\ H\ T\ U \\ 6\ 3\ 7\ 9 \\ -\ 1\ 2\ 4\ 6 \\ \hline \end{array}$$
$$\begin{array}{r} Th\ H\ T\ U \\ 6\ 3\ 7\ 9 \\ -\ 1\ 2\ 4\ 6 \\ \hline 5\ 1\ 3\ 3 \end{array}$$

1
$$\begin{array}{r} Th\ H\ T\ U \\ 4\ 9\ 2\ 6 \\ -\ 2\ 7\ 1\ 4 \\ \hline \end{array}$$

5
$$\begin{array}{r} Th\ H\ T\ U \\ 9\ 2\ 0\ 6 \\ -\ 1\ 0\ 0\ 5 \\ \hline \end{array}$$

2
$$\begin{array}{r} Th\ H\ T\ U \\ 7\ 6\ 2\ 9 \\ -\ 4\ 1\ 0\ 6 \\ \hline \end{array}$$

6
$$\begin{array}{r} Th\ H\ T\ U \\ 7\ 3\ 6\ 6 \\ -\ \ \ 1\ 5\ 4 \\ \hline \end{array}$$

3
$$\begin{array}{r} Th\ H\ T\ U \\ 5\ 9\ 6\ 3 \\ -\ 2\ 4\ 3\ 1 \\ \hline \end{array}$$

7
$$\begin{array}{r} Th\ H\ T\ U \\ 4\ 7\ 9\ 6 \\ -\ 2\ 3\ 9\ 1 \\ \hline \end{array}$$

4
$$\begin{array}{r} Th\ H\ T\ U \\ 5\ 2\ 7\ 3 \\ -\ \ \ 1\ 6\ 1 \\ \hline \end{array}$$

8
$$\begin{array}{r} Th\ H\ T\ U \\ 5\ 8\ 4\ 6 \\ -\ 4\ 7\ 4\ 5 \\ \hline \end{array}$$

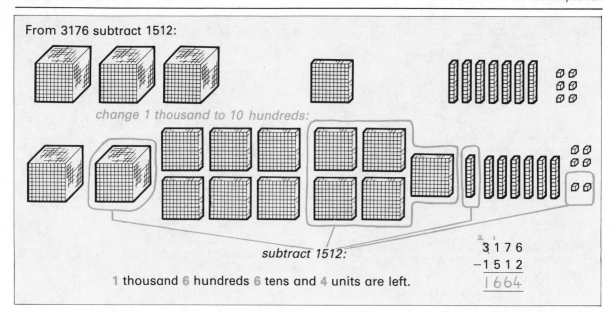

From 3176 subtract 1512:

change 1 thousand to 10 hundreds:

subtract 1512:

1 thousand 6 hundreds 6 tens and 4 units are left.

```
    2  1
  3 1 7 6
 -1 5 1 2
  ───────
  1 6 6 4
```

A Copy and complete:

```
☆   4 2 6 9        4 2 6 9
  - 1 6 3 2      - 1 6 3 2
    ───────        ───────
                   2 6 3 7
```

```
1   2 4 2 6      4   6 2 5 1
  - 1 6 2 1        - 4 7 2 1
```

```
2   6 1 9 5      5   5 8 6 8
  - 2 4 6 3        -   9 2 6
```

```
3   9 4 5 7      6   5 1 1 1
  - 2 8 3 0        - 1 5 0 1
```

B Copy and complete:

```
☆   3 6 5 4        3 6 5 4
  - 2 2 7 7      - 2 2 7 7
    ───────        ───────
                   1 3 7 7
```

```
1   3 8 5 7      3   3 6 2 8
  - 1 2 8 3        -   8 7 2
```

```
2   6 2 1 4      4   8 9 1 0
  - 3 8 0 3        - 3 9 7 1
```

mountain	height
Eiger	3970 m
Elbruz	5650 m
Ben Nevis	1344 m
Mont Blanc	4813 m
Ararat	5174 m

C What is the difference in height between:

☆ Elbruz and Eiger?

```
  5 6 5 0 m
- 3 9 7 0 m
  ─────────
  1 6 8 0 m
```

1 Ben Nevis and Mont Blanc?

2 Mont Blanc and Elbruz?

3 Eiger and Ben Nevis?

4 Ben Nevis and Ararat?

5 Elbruz and Ararat?

6 Mont Blanc and Ararat?

7 Eiger and Mont Blanc?

8 Ben Nevis and Elbruz?

Subtraction

From 6124
subtract 3376:

$$
\begin{array}{r}
^{5}\,^{10}\,^{11}\,^{1} \\
6\;1\;2\;4 \\
-3\;3\;7\;6 \\
\hline
2\;7\;4\;8
\end{array}
$$

A Copy and complete:

☆
$$
\begin{array}{r}
7\;1\;2\;6 \\
-3\;6\;5\;7 \\
\hline
\end{array}
\qquad
\begin{array}{r}
7\;1\;2\;6 \\
-3\;6\;5\;7 \\
\hline
3\;4\;6\;9
\end{array}
$$

1
$$
\begin{array}{r}
3\;8\;1\;2 \\
-1\;9\;9\;8 \\
\hline
\end{array}
$$

6
$$
\begin{array}{r}
3\;2\;8\;5 \\
-2\;6\;8\;6 \\
\hline
\end{array}
$$

2
$$
\begin{array}{r}
9\;2\;2\;3 \\
-1\;7\;9\;6 \\
\hline
\end{array}
$$

7
$$
\begin{array}{r}
8\;2\;3\;7 \\
-1\;4\;7\;9 \\
\hline
\end{array}
$$

3
$$
\begin{array}{r}
5\;3\;2\;6 \\
-2\;7\;8\;7 \\
\hline
\end{array}
$$

8
$$
\begin{array}{r}
3\;6\;2\;0 \\
-1\;9\;6\;1 \\
\hline
\end{array}
$$

4
$$
\begin{array}{r}
6\;6\;8\;4 \\
-\;\;\;9\;9\;5 \\
\hline
\end{array}
$$

9
$$
\begin{array}{r}
4\;3\;9\;2 \\
-2\;7\;9\;4 \\
\hline
\end{array}
$$

5
$$
\begin{array}{r}
7\;1\;5\;8 \\
-1\;6\;7\;9 \\
\hline
\end{array}
$$

10
$$
\begin{array}{r}
8\;0\;3\;7 \\
-5\;6\;3\;9 \\
\hline
\end{array}
$$

B What is the **difference** in cost between:

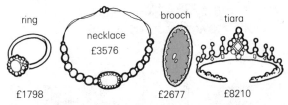

ring £1798
necklace £3576
brooch £2677
tiara £8210

☆ the brooch and the ring?
$$
\begin{array}{r}
£2\;6\;7\;7 \\
-£1\;7\;9\;8 \\
\hline
£\;\;\;8\;7\;9
\end{array}
$$

1 the brooch and the necklace?

2 the tiara and the ring?

3 the necklace and the tiara?

From 3000 subtract 1246:

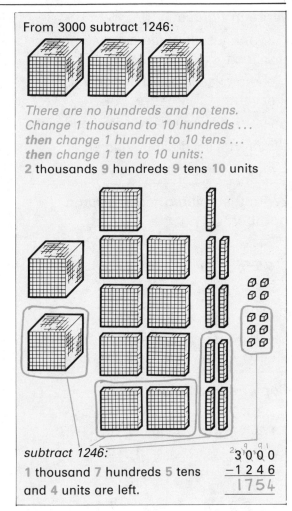

*There are no hundreds and no tens.
Change 1 thousand to 10 hundreds ...
then change 1 hundred to 10 tens ...
then change 1 ten to 10 units:*
2 thousands 9 hundreds 9 tens 10 units

subtract 1246:
1 thousand 7 hundreds 5 tens
and 4 units are left.

$$
\begin{array}{r}
^{2}\,^{9}\,^{9}\,^{1} \\
3\;0\;0\;0 \\
-1\;2\;4\;6 \\
\hline
1\;7\;5\;4
\end{array}
$$

C Use subtraction to answer these:

☆ Mr Saver has £1000 in the Bank. If he takes out £137, how much money does he have left in the bank?
$$
\begin{array}{r}
£1\;0\;0\;0 \\
-£\;\;\;1\;3\;7 \\
\hline
£\;\;\;8\;6\;3
\end{array}
$$

1 St John's Church needs £3000. If they collect £1376, how much more do they need?

2 What is the difference in cost between a car costing £5000 and a van costing £3950?

3 £5000−£2816= ✳

4 £3000−£1432= ✳

5 £8000−£2796= ✳

6 £6000−£3425= ✳

A Write in figures:

1 two thousand three hundred and sixteen
2 one thousand four hundred and seventy
3 five thousand one hundred and nine
4 four thousand eight hundred
5 nine thousand and twelve

B Write the value of each **orange** number:

1 241**6**
2 **4**385
3 2**9**7
4 1**6**2
5 320**4**
6 **6**411
7 27**5**3
8 4**2**26
9 1**8**7
10 51**6**2
11 451**9**
12 **7**333

C Copy and complete:

1 3 4 2 6
 +1 7 3 4

2 4 7 1 3
 +3 8 9 4

3 2 1 3 6
 + 9 9 6

4 1 3 7 5
 + 4 8 7

5 1 6 9 6
 +3 2 7 5

6 2 1 9 4
   3 2 1
 +1 6 3 6

7   2 1 6
   4 3 3 0
 + 4 7 2

8 1 4 9 3
 +1 4 9 6

9 2 4 6 8
   1 2 3 4
 + 1 9 9

D Add together:

1 27, 62 and 49
2 36, 54 and 27
3 46, 29 and 15
4 37, 47 and 57
5 16, 29 and 87
6 98, 16 and 59

E Copy and complete:

1 2 3 7 5
 −1 2 8 2

2 4 1 2 6
 − 3 8 2

3 6 8 1 9
 −4 2 9 9

4 3 8 7 3
 −1 4 9 5

5 6 2 1 7
 −1 4 0 8

6 3 6 2 4
 −1 7 5 5

7 4 3 7 6
 −2 3 7 9

8 8 9 1 0
 −6 8 9 1

9 4 6 3 4
 −1 7 1 8

10 5 1 0 9
 −2 4 6 3

F Answer these questions:

1 Jason has 1294 stamps and Alice has 2162 stamps. How many more stamps has Alice than Jason?

2 In a 3000 metre race, Steve has run 1635 metres. How far has he still to run?

3 A school raises £1698 at a Summer Fair and £1294 from a sponsored walk. How much money is raised altogether?

4 655 people visit a fair in the morning, 1320 go during the afternoon and 1369 go during the evening. How many people visit the fair altogether?

A You need: nine cards numbered 1 to 9, 2 dice numbered 1 to 6 and a partner.

Lay out the cards in order: 1 2 3 4 5 6 7 8 9

Throw the two dice.

Turn over cards to match the total of your throw.

For example: Throw ⚅ ⚀ You can turn 1 5 or 2 4 or 1 2 3 or 6 .

Continue rolling the dice until you cannot match your throw.

When this happens your turn has ended and your score is shown by the remaining cards.

Examples ▢ ▢ 3 ▢ ▢ 6 7 ▢ ▢   score **367**

1 2 ▢ ▢ ▢ 6 ▢ 8 ▢   score **1268**

Your partner now has a turn.

The player with the lowest total score after 5 games wins the match.

Investigate what effect it has on the game if the cards are laid out in reverse order.

Is the game improved if: a) less cards are laid out?
b) a player can choose to use 1 or 2 dice at each turn?

B Take any 3-figure number...   **815**
Reverse the digits...   **518**
Add the two numbers together...   1333
Reverse the digits in the answer...   **3331**
Add this number to the first answer...   **4664**

This number reads the same backwards and forwards. It is called a **PALINDROME**.

In this example the digits were reversed and added **twice** before a palindromic number was found. From the number **815** you can find the palindromic number in **2 stages**.

Find how many stages you need to find a palindromic number from the number a) 138   b) 482

Find 3 more numbers that make a palindromic number in
a) 1 stage   b) 2 stages   c) 3 stages

Can you find any 3-digit numbers that do not lead to palindromic numbers?

Answer any questions you can. Leave those you cannot do.
You should not use a calculator for the questions on this page.

1 Write in figures two thousand three hundred and fourteen.

2 Write in figures five thousand and eleven.

Using the figures 1, 5, 6 and 8 make a number that is:

3 between five thousand and five thousand five hundred.

4 greater than six thousand but less than six thousand five hundred.

How many candles do you need to make up:

5 eighteen boxes of ten candles?

6 eighty-three boxes of ten candles?

7 two hundred and ninety-one boxes of ten candles?

8 one thousand one hundred boxes of ten candles?

How many packs of 100 counters can you make from:

9 1200 counters?

10 5900 counters?

11 8200 counters?

Copy and complete:

12
```
   3 6
   2 7
 + 4 9
```

13
```
   5 6 8
   1 2 9
 + 1 4 5
```

14
```
   1 6 9 2
 + 4 1 0 7
```

15
```
   3 7 2 9
 + 1 6 4 0
```

16
```
   5 6 2 4
 + 2 7 9 1
```

17
```
   3 6 9 8
 + 2 4 0 3
```

18
```
   4 6 2 7
 + 2 9 9 6
```

19 By 2.30 pm 4261 spectators had arrived for a football match.
If 2688 spectators arrived after 2.30 pm how many spectators were there altogether?

20 Mr. Lotsovcash buys 2 cars costing £4968 and £3879. How much does he spend altogether?

Copy and complete:

21
```
   5 4 7 6
 - 2 2 5 4
```

22
```
   4 0 9 3
 - 1 2 3 2
```

23
```
   8 6 8 3
 - 2 7 9 0
```

24
```
   4 4 4 4
 - 1 0 5 5
```

25
```
   8 6 2 4
 - 5 7 9 7
```

26 Two rings cost £3972 and £1586. What is the difference in the prices?

27 Winston swims 2500 metres and Abigail swims 965 metres. How much further does Winston swim than Abigail?

Time

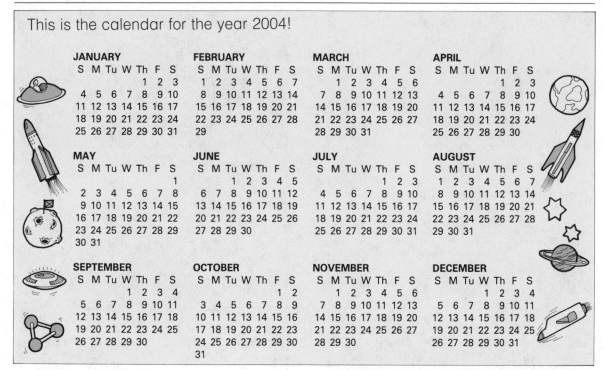

This is the calendar for the year 2004!

A Use the **calendar** to answer these:

1 Write the months that have 30 days.
2 In 2004, how many days in February?
3 Is 2004 a leap year?
4 Write the months that have 31 days.
5 How many days in 2004?
6 How many days in a leap year?

B In 2004, what **date** is:

☆ the first Wednesday in October?
   October 6th
1 the third Sunday in August?
2 the last Saturday in July?
3 the sixth Saturday of the year?
4 the last Monday of the year?
5 two weeks after June 12th?
6 1 week before April 4th?
7 10 days before November 9th?
8 21 days after July 29th?
9 two weeks after August 18th?
10 five weeks before October 6th?

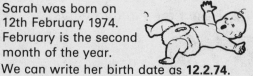
Sarah was born on 12th February 1974. February is the second month of the year. We can write her birth date as **12.2.74.**

C Write these **dates** in figures:

☆ 9th June 1982   9.6.82
1 5th May 1980
2 16th January 1973
3 18th December 1960
4 20th June 1955
5 27th February 1983
6 your birth date
7 tomorrow's date
8 yesterday's date

D What is the **day**:

☆ 1 week after 6.8.04?   Friday
1 4 days after 7.10.04?
2 10 days after 1.4.04?
3 1 week after 19.12.04?
4 21 days after 28.2.04?
5 28 days before 16.6.04?

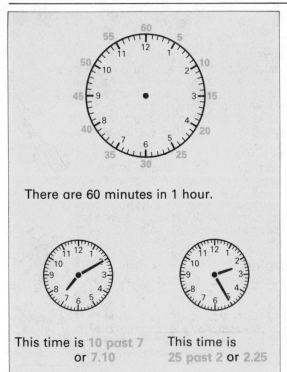

There are 60 minutes in 1 hour.

This time is 10 past 7 or 7.10

This time is 25 past 2 or 2.25

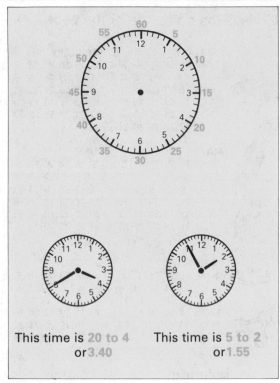

This time is 20 to 4 or 3.40

This time is 5 to 2 or 1.55

A Write these **times** in two ways:

☆ 5 past 8
8.05

1 3 5

2 4 6

B Write these **times** in figures:

☆ quarter past six   6.15

1 20 past 9   4 quarter past 3

2 5 past 12   5 half past 7

3 25 past 10   6 3 o'clock

C Write these **times** in two ways:

☆ 10 to 5
4.50

1 3 5

2 4 6

D Write these **times** in figures:

☆ quarter to eight   7.45

1 10 to 7   4 25 to 1

2 20 to 9   5 5 to 11

3 quarter to 3   6 10 to 10

Time

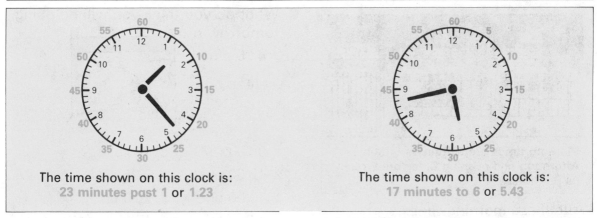

The time shown on this clock is:
23 minutes past 1 or **1.23**

The time shown on this clock is:
17 minutes to 6 or **5.43**

A Write these **times** in 2 different ways:

☆
12 minutes past 3
3.12

1

2

3

4

5

6

7

8

B Write these **times** in 2 different ways:

☆
8 minutes to 4
3.52

1

2

3

4

5

6

7

8

Morning times are written as am times.
Afternoon and evening times are written
as pm times.

A Write these **morning times**:

☆ 4.15 am

B Write these **afternoon** and **evening times**:

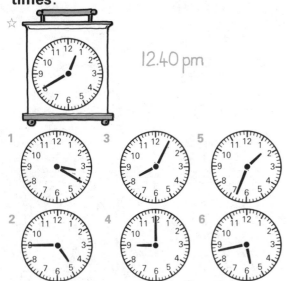

☆ 12.40 pm

C What do you think you will be doing tomorrow at:

☆ 4.00 am?

sleeping

1	9.00 am?	6	10.45 am?
2	12.30 pm?	7	8.25 am?
3	10.00 pm?	8	2.30 pm?
4	6.30 pm?	9	12.00 am (midday)?
5	8.30 pm?	10	12.00 pm (midnight)?

D What time will it be 3 hours after these morning times?

☆ 6 am   9 am

1	2 am	6	6 am
2	4 am	7	3 am
3	9 am	8	10 am
4	1 am	9	11 am
5	5 am	10	7 am

E What time will it be $\frac{1}{2}$ hour after these afternoon and evening times?

☆ 5 pm   5.30 pm

1	4.00 pm	6	12.50 pm
2	7.30 pm	7	8.42 pm
3	9.30 pm	8	6.23 pm
4	8.15 pm	9	1.02 pm
5	12.20 pm	10	3.30 pm

F What time will it be 10 minutes after these morning times?

☆ 3.20 am   3.30 am

1	6.15 am	6	12.50 am
2	8.40 am	7	9.08 am
3	7.50 am	8	4.53 am
4	4.15 am	9	12.04 am
5	1.55 am	10	11.51 am

Time

A Use a clock face if you need to.
For how long was:

starting time   finishing time

☆ Jill walking to
   the bus stop?

25 minutes

1 Mrs Hill working?

2 Mr Adams driving?

3 Mrs Ingram shopping?

4 Jack climbing?

B Write the time that is:

☆ 10 minutes later than 4.27 pm 4.37 pm
1 10 minutes later than 6.35 pm
2 20 minutes later than 2.12 pm
3 10 minutes earlier than 4.16 am
4 15 minutes earlier than 9.23 pm
5 12 minutes later than 10.04 am
6 16 minutes earlier than 7.28 am
7 22 minutes later than 8.17 pm
8 17 minutes earlier than 5.20 am
9 24 minutes later than 4.52 pm
10 11 minutes earlier than 1.04 am

C Answer these questions:

☆ It takes John twenty minutes to walk
   to school. If he arrives at 8.45 am, at
   what time did he set out? 8.25 am

1 Mrs Jackson wants her cake to be
   ready at 4.00 pm. If the cake takes
   40 minutes to cook, at what time
   must it be put in the oven?

2 Mr Bone's car journey takes 1 hour
   and 10 minutes. If he arrives at
   10.30 am, at what time did he leave?

3 Ben Trotter ran the London marathon
   in 3 hours 45 minutes. If he
   finished running at 4.15 pm,
   at what time did
   he start?

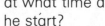

bus timetable			
	bus 1	bus 2	bus 3
Oxford	7.30 am	11.25 am	3.10 pm
Kennington	7.42 am	11.37 am	3.12 pm
Radley	7.51 am	11.46 am	3.21 pm
Abingdon	7.58 am	11.54 am	3.28 pm
Culham	8.08 am	12.05 pm	3.38 pm
Dorchester	8.20 am	12.18 pm	3.50 pm

A Use the bus timetable to answer these questions:

☆ How long does bus 1 take to travel from Radley to Culham? *17 minutes*

1 How long does bus 2 take to travel from Abingdon to Dorchester?

2 How long does bus 3 take for the whole journey from Oxford to Dorchester?

3 How long after bus 1 leaves Oxford, does bus 2 leave Oxford?

4 How long does bus 1 take to travel from Kennington to Dorchester?

5 You are ready to leave Radley at 11.39 am. How long will you have to wait for bus 2?

6 If you need to be in Culham at 2.30 pm, which bus would you catch from Oxford?

7 Which bus takes the longest time to complete the journey from Oxford to Dorchester?

train timetable		
	train 1	train 2
London	9.35 am	10.35 am
Southampton	10.43 am	11.42 am
Bournemouth	11.17 am	12.17 pm
Wareham	11.42 am	12.42 pm
Dorchester	12.06 pm	1.06 pm
Weymouth	12.17 pm	1.17 pm

B Use the train timetable to answer these questions:

☆ How long does train 1 take to travel from London to Wareham?
2 hours 7 minutes

1 How long does train 2 take to travel from Bournemouth to Weymouth?

2 How long does train 1 take to travel from London to Bournemouth?

3 How long does train 1 take for the whole journey from London to Weymouth?

4 How long does train 2 take for the whole journey?

5 When train 1 is in Wareham, where is train 2?

6 When train 2 is in Bournemouth, where is train 1?

7 Which train takes longer to travel from Southampton to Bournemouth?

8 Which train would you catch to be in Dorchester by 1.00 pm?

9 If you need to be in Weymouth at half past one in the afternoon, which train would you catch?

A Write these dates in figures:

1 15th July 1966
2 24th May 1980
3 14th August 1983
4 1st December 1984
5 25th September 1941
6 13th April 1979
7 4th February 1976
8 29th October 1915

B Write these times in 2 ways:

1
5
9

2
6
10

3
7
11

4
8
12

C Write these times in figures:

1 20 past 7
2 half past 12
3 10 to 6
4 quarter to 8
5 quarter past 3
6 5 to 10
7 9 o'clock
8 25 to 6
9 20 to 2
10 25 past 11

D For how long was:

starting time   finishing time

1 Ivor Pain weeding?
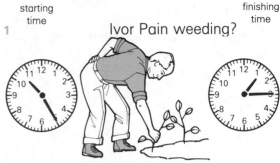

2 Mr Harris mowing?

3 Linda flying?

4 Grandpa cycling?

E Write the time that is:

1 10 minutes earlier than 4.25 am
2 30 minutes later than 6.10 pm
3 25 minutes earlier than 4.20 pm
4 40 minutes later than 5.50 am
5 $\frac{1}{2}$ an hour later than 10.55 pm
6 45 minutes earlier than 1.20 am

A Here is part of a time chain for a day in the life of a fisherman.

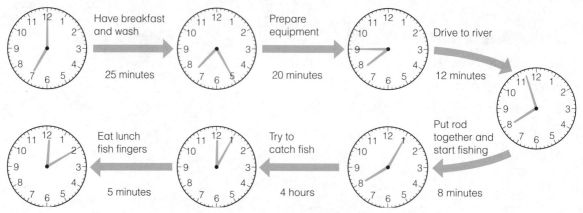

Have breakfast and wash — 25 minutes
Prepare equipment — 20 minutes
Drive to river — 12 minutes
Put rod together and start fishing — 8 minutes
Try to catch fish — 4 hours
Eat lunch fish fingers — 5 minutes

Draw a time chain for yourself for one day of your life.

B Some dates are **palindromic**. This means that they read the same backwards and forwards.

For example: 24.9.42.

Here are two more palindromic dates: 16.11.61. 4.2.24.

How many palindromic dates can you find in the year 1962?

How many palindromic dates have there been since 1st January 1900?

C Try this time game. You will need a stop watch, 2 sets of ten counters and a partner.

The first player chooses a square which shows a period of time. Using the stop watch, each player times the other player as they estimate the passing of this length of time. The player with the closer estimate covers the square with a coloured counter.

Players take turns in this way until the winning player has a straight line of 3 counters together or all ten counters on the board.

Try to find a method for estimating accurately the passing of one minute. You might recite a poem or simply count.

Is counting your pulse a good method for estimating periods of time?

50 seconds	25 seconds	2 minutes	$\frac{1}{4}$ minute
$1\frac{1}{4}$ minutes	$\frac{1}{2}$ minute	30 seconds	40 seconds
15 seconds	45 seconds	20 seconds	15 seconds
1 minute	35 seconds	10 seconds	$1\frac{1}{2}$ minutes

Answer any questions you can. Leave those you cannot do.

1 How many days in April?

2 How many days in October?

3 How many days in November?

4 How many days in a fortnight?

5 How many days in a year?

6 How many days in a leap year?

Here is part of the calendar for the year 2008.

April						May						June					
M		7	14	21	28	M		5	12	19	26	M		2	9	16	23	30
T	1	8	15	22	29	T		6	13	20	27	T		3	10	17	24
W	2	9	16	23	30	W		7	14	21	28	W		4	11	18	25
T	3	10	17	24		T	1	8	15	22	29	T		5	12	19	26
F	4	11	18	25		F	2	9	16	23	30	F		6	13	20	27
S	5	12	19	26		S	3	10	17	24	31	S		7	14	21	28
S	6	13	20	27		S	4	11	18	25		S	1	8	15	22	29

7 On what day is 18th May?

8 What day of the week is 16 days after 4th June?

9 What is the date of the first Sunday in July?

10 On what day is March 1st?

11 On what day is August 7th?

Write these dates in figures:

12 28th July 1964

13 14th April 1982

14 15th March 1926.

Choose the correct answer A, B or C.

15

This time can be written as:

A 5.46   B 9.25

C 10.25

16 20 to 6 can be written as:

A 6.40   B 6.22   C 5.40.

17 7.22 can be written as:

A twenty-two minutes to seven.

B twenty-two minutes past seven.

C seven minutes past ten.

Write these times in figures.

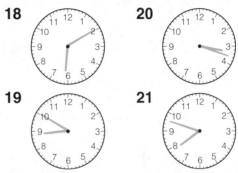

18   **20**

19   **21**

How long did these journeys take?

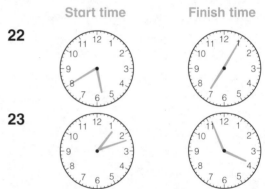

	Start time	Finish time
22		
23		

24 Jacky's cycle ride finished at 2.07 pm.

If the ride took 50 minutes, at what time did she start?

25 What time is 3 hours and nineteen minutes later than 1.45 am?

26 How many seconds in one minute?

27 How many seconds in $\frac{1}{4}$ minute?

28 How many seconds in five minutes?

These are the times for a 200 m race:

Billy	39.87 seconds.
Hassan	32.39 seconds.
Jack	35.73 seconds.
Mike	32.51 seconds.

29 Who was the winner of the race?

30 Who had the slowest time?

Spy trails

Write the word at the end of each spy trail to see who robbed the bank.

Start at A. Follow this trail:
8×8 6×8 7×4 6×6 8×9 10×5

Write: *the*

Start at B. Follow this trail:
9×4 6×3 9×9 8×5 6×7 10×8 6×5

Start at C. Follow this trail:
7×5 7×8 3×10 4×8 7×7 6×9 10×7 9×2

Start at D. Follow this trail:
5×4 3×8 5×5 5×6 10×10 6×6 8×7 9×5

Start at E. Follow this trail:
9×3 7×5 6×4 8×8 7×10 5×8 9×6 2×8

Start at F. Follow this trail:
8×4 7×7 4×4 8×8 6×6 5×9 7×9 10×4

Suspects

A			B				C		
64	42	32	30	36	12	hair	30	35	54
48	28	36	with	18	70	54	50	56	28
24	70	72	64	81	hat	49	32	30	36
black	60	50	36	40	42	80	63	coat	27
33	18	the	48	72	100	30	25	24	20
ora-nge	16	54	40	20	36	man	60	eyes	36
30	48	the	70	nose	56	42	54	64	12
32	49	16	64	36	45	63	40	tie	24
25	coat	90	24	35	the	72	56	80	28
27	18	14	33	27	39	81	lady	27	45

D (right side, row 5)

F (left side, row 8)

E (bottom)

Multiplication

Multiply 146 by 2:

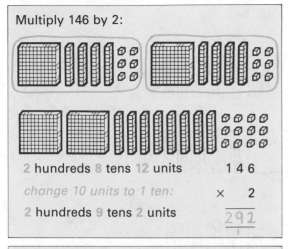

2 hundreds **8** tens **12** units   1 4 6

change 10 units to 1 ten: ×   2

2 hundreds **9** tens **2** units   2̲9̲2̲
                             1

Multiply 162 by 2:

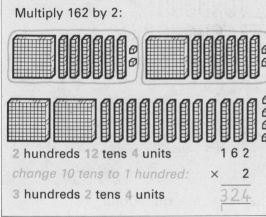

2 hundreds **12** tens **4** units   1 6 2

change 10 tens to 1 hundred: ×   2

3 hundreds **2** tens **4** units   3̲2̲4̲
                            1

Multiply 138 by 3:

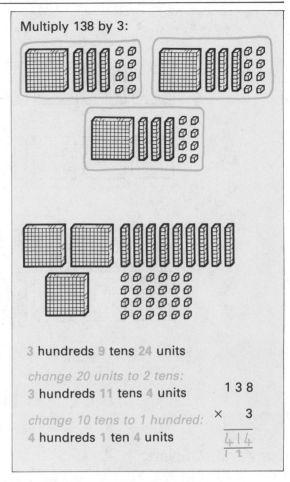

3 hundreds **9** tens **24** units

change 20 units to 2 tens:
3 hundreds **11** tens **4** units   1 3 8

change 10 tens to 1 hundred: ×   3

4 hundreds **1** ten **4** units   4̲1̲4̲
                           1 1

A Use apparatus if you need to.
Copy and complete:

☆   1 4 3   1 4 3
  ×   3   ×   3
  ‾‾‾‾‾   4̲2̲9̲

1   2 4 7   5   2 9 3   9   2 6 0
   ×   2   ×   2   ×   3

2   1 2 4   6   1 1 8   10   2 6 1
   ×   4   ×   2   ×   3

3   2 5 3   7   2 0 3   11   1 2 3
   ×   3   ×   4   ×   4

4   1 5 2   8   1 1 3   12   1 3 1
   ×   3   ×   5   ×   5

B Use apparatus if you need to.
Copy and complete:

☆   2 3 7   2 3 7
  ×   4   ×   4
  ‾‾‾‾‾   9̲4̲8̲

1   1 2 6   5   1 3 4   9   1 2 7
   ×   4   ×   5   ×   5

2   1 3 5   6   2 4 9   10   1 2 3
   ×   5   ×   3   ×   8

3   1 4 7   7   1 0 6   11   3 6
   ×   3   ×   4   ×   5

4   2 1 8   8   2 0 7   12   1 5 8
   ×   3   ×   4   ×   4

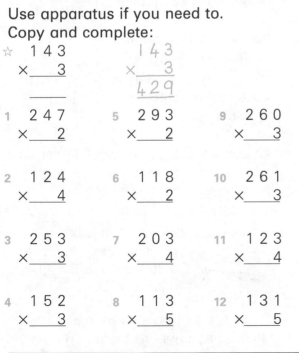

Multiply 564 by 2:

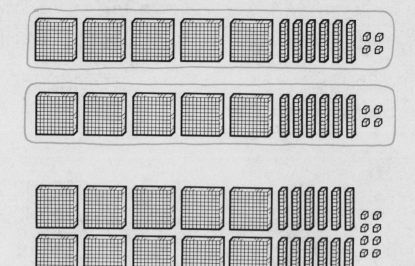

10 hundreds 12 tens 8 units
change 10 tens to 1 hundred:
11 hundreds 2 tens 8 units
change 10 hundreds to 1 thousand:
1 thousand 1 hundred 2 tens 8 units

```
      5 6 4
  ×       2
    1 1 2 8
    1 1
```

A Copy and complete:

```
☆     3 5 3          3 5 3
  ×       5      ×       5
                   1 7 6 5
```

```
1     2 5 2    6     4 2 6    11    2 3 2
  ×       4      ×       4      ×       6
```

```
2     3 2 5    7     1 2 2    12    2 2 2
  ×       5      ×       9      ×       5
```

```
3     6 2 3    8     3 6 6    13    2 3 5
  ×       3      ×       4      ×       7
```

```
4     5 4 9    9     2 4 3    14    3 6 4
  ×       2      ×       6      ×       5
```

```
5     1 5 3    10    2 5 4    15    2 8 7
  ×       7      ×       4      ×       4
```

B Answer these questions:

☆ If there are 124 paint
brushes in each box,
how many brushes are
there in 4 boxes?

```
    1 2 4
  ×     4
    4 9 6
```

1 Rubber spiders cost 26p each.
What is the cost of 4 spiders?

2 Chairs were put in rows of 13 for the
school play. If there were 9 rows,
how many chairs were there
altogether?

3 If there are 224 pages in a book,
 how many pages will
there be in 5 of these
books?

4 There are 144 bars of soap in a box.
How many bars are there in 6 boxes?

Multiplication

To **multiply** a number by **10,** move the number one column to the **left**:

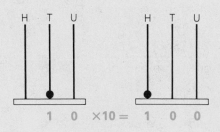 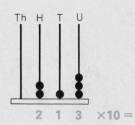 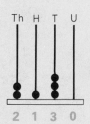

A Write numbers for ✷'s:

✰ 7×10=✷   70

1   8×10=✷   6   10×6=✷
2   10×8=✷   7   9×10=✷
3   4×10=✷   8   10×9=✷
4   10×4=✷   9   3×10=✷
5   6×10=✷   10   10×3=✷

B **Multiply** the number shown on each abacus by **10.** Draw an abacus to show each answer:

✰ 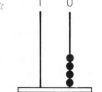   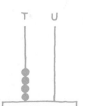

1 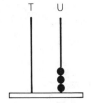   3

2   4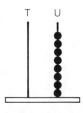

C **Multiply** the number shown on each abacus by **10.**
Draw an abacus to show your answer:

✰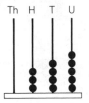

1   3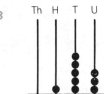

2   4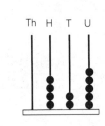

D Write answers only:

✰ 39×10=✷   390

1   11×10=✷   5   121×10=✷
2   13×10=✷   6   143×10=✷
3   22×10=✷   7   276×10=✷
4   74×10=✷   8   842×10=✷

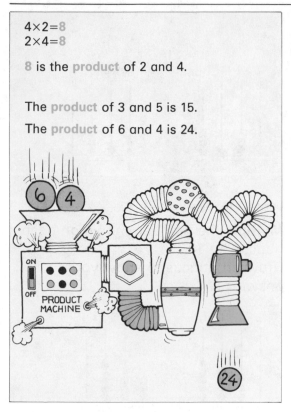

$4 \times 2 = 8$
$2 \times 4 = 8$

8 is the product of 2 and 4.

The product of 3 and 5 is 15.
The product of 6 and 4 is 24.

$3 \times 4 = 12$
$4 \times 3 = 12$

3 and 4 are factors of 12.

$2 \times 6 = 12$
$6 \times 2 = 12$

2 and 6 are also factors of 12.

$1 \times 12 = 12$
$12 \times 1 = 12$

1 and 12 are also factors of 12.
The factors of 12 are: 1, 2, 3, 4, 6, 12.

A Write the **product** of:

☆ 3 and 7   21

1 4 and 5
2 3 and 9
3 5 and 6
4 6 and 7
5 2 and 10

6 7 and 8
7 9 and 4
8 5 and 8
9 9 and 6
10 5 and 9

B What is the **product** of:

☆ thirty-four and five?

$$\begin{array}{r} 34 \\ \times\ \ 5 \\ \hline 170 \end{array}$$

1 twenty-seven and four?
2 forty-nine and three?
3 thirteen and eight?
4 sixty-four and six?
5 fifty-three and three?
6 twenty-one and nine?

C Copy and complete:

☆ $3 \times \ast = 15$ $3 \times 5 = 15$
   $\ast \times 3 = 15$ $5 \times 3 = 15$
   $1 \times \ast = 15$ $1 \times 15 = 15$
   $\ast \times 1 = 15$ $15 \times 1 = 15$

1 $3 \times \ast = 18$
   $\ast \times 3 = 18$
   $2 \times \ast = 18$
   $\ast \times 2 = 18$
   $1 \times \ast = 18$
   $\ast \times 1 = 18$

2 $2 \times \ast = 10$
   $5 \times \ast = 10$
   $1 \times \ast = 10$
   $\ast \times 1 = 10$

3 $4 \times \ast = 20$
   $\ast \times 4 = 20$
   $2 \times \ast = 20$
   $\ast \times 2 = 20$
   $1 \times \ast = 20$
   $\ast \times 1 = 20$

4 $3 \times \ast = 21$
   $\ast \times 3 = 21$
   $1 \times \ast = 21$
   $\ast \times 1 = 21$

D Write the **factors** of:

☆ 18   1, 2, 3, 6, 9, 18

1 15
2 10
3 20

4 21
5 8
6 6

7 14
8 22
9 24

Number

4×4=16
16 has two equal factors.
When a number has 2 equal factors,
the number is a square number.

Here is a square pattern
made with 16 dots:
4×4=16   16 is a square number.

Here is a square pattern
made with 9 dots:
3×3=9   9 is a square number.

With 12 dots, you can form different
rectangle patterns:

From these patterns you can see that:

2×6=12   6×2=12

4×3=12   3×4=12

12 is a rectangular number

A Write the **square numbers** shown by
these dot patterns:

☆ **::**   4

1

2

3

B On squared paper, draw a square
dot pattern for these numbers.
Show the **2 equal factors:**

☆ 25   5×5=25

1 36   2 81   3 100

C Draw one rectangle pattern for each
of these numbers:

☆ 15

1 6   4 10   7 27

2 8   5 21   8 28

3 18   6 14   9 22

D Write 2 multiplication facts for each
of these rectangles:

☆ 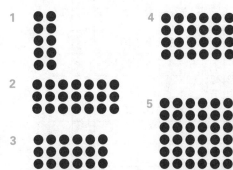   4×6=24
                           6×4=24

1

4

2

5

3

A Copy and complete this multiplication square on **centimetre squared** paper:

X	1	2	3	4	5	6	7	8	9	10
1		2								
2			6				14			
3										
4		8			20					40
5										
6			18						54	
7						42				
8										
9				36				72		
10	10									

B You need some counters.

1 Write down the **square numbers** from 1 to 100.

2 Use counters to cover the square numbers on your multiplication square.

3 Do the counters form a symmetrical pattern on your square?

C 1 Copy and complete this pattern on **centimetre squared** paper.

2 Shade in the square numbers.

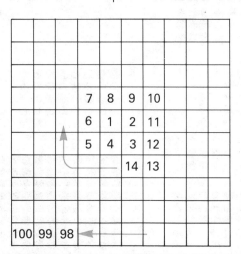

This pattern of numbers is part of a **multiplication square**.

2	3	4
4	6	8
6	9	12
8	12	16

What are the **products** of the numbers in the opposite corners of the pattern?

```
  1 6          8
× _ 2        × 4
  3 2         3 2
```

D Find these sections on a multiplication square. Draw lines round each one. Work out the **products** of the numbers in opposite corners:

☆

5	6	7
10	12	14
15	18	21
20	24	28

```
  20
×  7
 140

  28
×  5
 140
```

1

7	14	21	28
8	16	24	32
9	18	27	36

4

6	7	8	9	10
12	14	16	18	20
18	21	24	27	30

2

3	6	9	12	15
4	8	12	16	20
5	10	15	20	25

5

9	18	27	36	45
10	20	30	40	50

3

7	8	9
14	16	18
21	24	27
28	32	36
35	40	45

6

2	4	6	8	10	12
3	6	9	12	15	18
4	8	12	16	20	24
5	10	15	20	25	30
6	12	18	24	30	36
7	14	21	28	35	42

A **multiplication square** can help with division:

Sausages are packed in eights. How many packs can be made with 48 sausages?

For 48÷8= ✳ **say:**
'how many eights are there in 48?'

The square shows that 6 eights=48.
48÷8=6   6 packs can be made.

X	1	2	3	4	5	6	7	8	9	10
1	1	2	3	4	5	6	7	8	9	10
2	2	4	6	8	10	12	14	16	18	20
3	3	6	9	12	15	18	21	24	27	30
4	4	8	12	16	20	24	28	32	36	40
5	5	10	15	20	25	30	35	40	45	50
6	6	12	18	24	30	36	42	48	54	60
7	7	14	21	28	35	42	49	56	63	70
8	8	16	24	32	40	48	56	64	72	80
9	9	18	27	36	45	54	63	72	81	90
10	10	20	30	40	50	60	70	80	90	100

A Use the multiplication square to help you answer these:

☆ Toys are packed 8 to a box. How many boxes will be needed to pack 72 toys?   9

1 How many sixes are there in 54?

2 How many nines are there in 45?

3 How many tens are there in 80?

4 How many sevens are there in 63?

5 Pencils are packed in tens. How many packs can be made with 70 pencils?

6 How many bunches of 9 flowers each can be made with 81 flowers?

7 There are 7 girls in a netball team. How many teams can be made with 49 girls?

8 Lorries have eight wheels. How many lorries can be fitted with 56 wheels?

B Use the multiplication square. Write numbers for ✳'s:

☆ 45÷9= ✳   5

1 64÷8= ✳

2 56÷7= ✳

3 32÷8= ✳

4 90÷10= ✳

5 16÷4= ✳

6 28÷4= ✳

7 45÷5= ✳

8 30÷6= ✳

9 36÷6= ✳

10 63÷9= ✳

11 49÷7= ✳

12 81÷9= ✳

13 30÷5= ✳

14 100÷10= ✳

C Use the multiplication square. Write numbers for ✳'s:

☆ **28÷ ✳ =7**   4

X	1	2	3	4	5	6	7
1	1	2	3	4	5	6	7
2	2	4	6	8	10	12	14
3	3	6	9	12	15	18	21
4	4	8	12	16	20	24	28

1 12÷ ✳ =3

2 18÷ ✳ =6

3 32÷ ✳ =8

4 25÷ ✳ =5

5 64÷ ✳ =8

6 100÷ ✳ =10

7 56÷ ✳ =8

8 49÷ ✳ =7

9 42÷ ✳ =6

10 90÷ ✳ =10

11 45÷ ✳ =9

12 54÷ ✳ =6

13 81÷ ✳ =9

14 60÷ ✳ =6

Follow wires with correct answers. Which object is turned
on by the **start** switch?

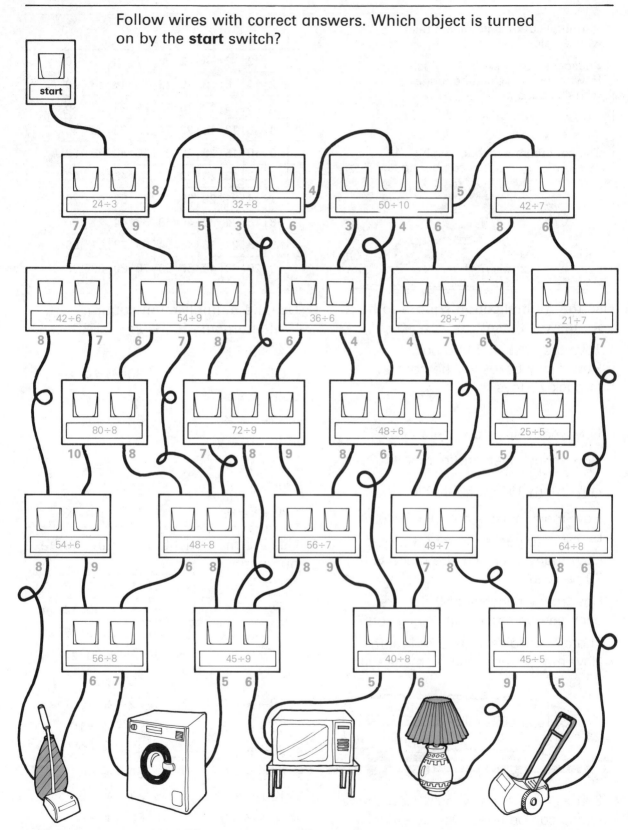

Division

X	1	2	3	4	5	6	7	8	9	10
1	1	2	3	4	5	6	7	8	9	10
2	2	4	6	8	10	12	14	16	18	20
3	3	6	9	12	15	18	21	24	27	30
4	4	8	12	16	20	24	28	32	36	40
5	5	10	15	20	25	30	35	40	45	50
6	6	12	18	24	30	36	42	48	54	60
7	7	14	21	28	35	42	49	56	63	70
8	8	16	24	32	40	48	56	64	72	80
9	9	18	27	36	45	54	63	72	81	90
10	10	20	30	40	50	60	70	80	90	100

A Use the multiplication square to answer these:

☆ $60 \div 10 =$ ✷   6

1 $72 \div 8 =$ ✷   6 $42 \div 6 =$ ✷

2 $54 \div 6 =$ ✷   7 $50 \div 5 =$ ✷

3 $81 \div 9 =$ ✷   8 $28 \div 4 =$ ✷

4 $27 \div 3 =$ ✷   9 $63 \div 9 =$ ✷

5 $35 \div 7 =$ ✷   10 $49 \div 7 =$ ✷

B **Divide** the number shown on each abacus **by 10**. Draw an abacus to show each answer:

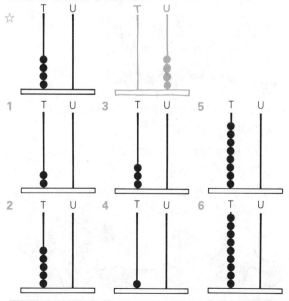

To divide a number **by 10,** move the number one column to the **right.**

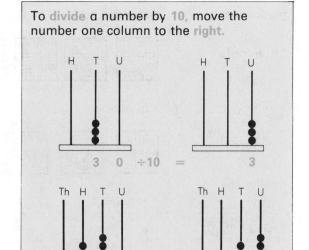

$3 \quad 0 \div 10 = 3$

$1 \quad 4 \quad 5 \quad 0 \div 10 = 1 \quad 4 \quad 5$

C **Divide** the number shown on each abacus **by 10**. Draw an abacus to show your answer:

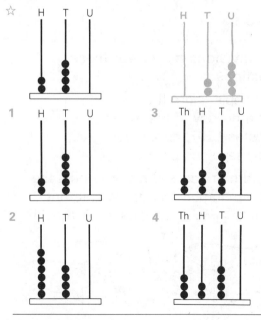

D Write answers only:

☆ $650 \div 10 =$ ✷   65

1 $230 \div 10 =$ ✷   4 $1260 \div 10 =$ ✷

2 $410 \div 10 =$ ✷   5 $3200 \div 10 =$ ✷

3 $650 \div 10 =$ ✷   6 $1060 \div 10 =$ ✷

Divide 369 by 3:

3 hundreds ÷ 3

6 tens ÷ 3

9 units ÷ 3

1 hundred
2 tens
3 units

```
  123
3)369
```

Divide 487 by 4:

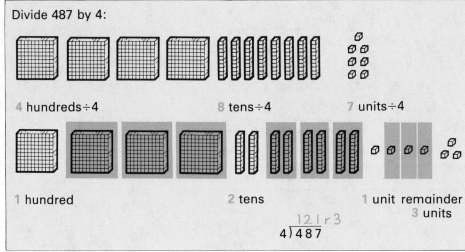

4 hundreds÷4   8 tens÷4   7 units÷4

1 hundred   2 tens   1 unit remainder
3 units

```
 121 r3
4)487
```

A Copy and complete:

☆ 4)480
```
  120
4)480
```

1 5)550   5 3)963

2 3)630   6 2)884

3 4)484   7 5)505

4 2)846   8 4)804

C Copy and complete:

☆ 6)605
```
  100 r5
6)605
```

1 2)483   5 8)881

2 4)407   6 2)629

3 5)559   7 4)446

4 3)962   8 3)998

B Use divisions to answer these questions:

☆ 7 people share the cost of a holiday. If the total cost is £707, how much do they each pay?

```
  £101
7)£707
```

1 A farmer has 360 pigs. He puts the same number into three different fields. How many pigs in each field?

2 Cakes are packed in fours. How many packs can be made with 480 cakes?

3 2 batsmen score 242 runs. If they each score the same number, how many runs does each man score?

D Answer these questions. How many each, and how many left over when:

☆ 394 chickens are shared equally among 3 farmers?

```
  131 r1
3)394
131 each
1 left over
```

1 409 flowers are shared equally among 4 people?

2 669 newspapers are shared equally among 6 shops?

3 503 custard pies are shared equally among 5 clowns?

Division

Divide 278 by 2: 2⟌2̄7̄8̄

divide 2 hundreds by 2: 2⟌2̄7̄8̄ (1)

divide 7 tens by 2: 2⟌2̄7̄8̄ (13)

divide 8 units by 2: 2⟌2̄7̄8̄ (139)

278÷2=139

Divide 568 by 4: 4⟌5̄6̄8̄

divide 5 hundreds by 4: 4⟌5̄6̄8̄ (1)

divide 6 tens by 4: 4⟌5̄6̄8̄ (14)

divide 8 units by 4: 4⟌5̄6̄8̄ (142)

568÷4=142

A Copy and complete:

☆ 5⟌5̄7̄5̄   5⟌5̄7̄5̄ (115)

1 4⟌4̄9̄6̄   4 7⟌7̄9̄1̄

2 5⟌5̄6̄0̄   5 4⟌4̄1̄2̄

3 3⟌9̄4̄5̄   6 2⟌8̄5̄6̄

C Copy and complete:

☆ 6⟌8̄4̄6̄   6⟌8̄4̄6̄ (141)

1 4⟌5̄2̄4̄   4 3⟌5̄7̄6̄

2 5⟌6̄5̄5̄   5 2⟌5̄6̄8̄

3 8⟌9̄6̄0̄   6 7⟌9̄1̄7̄

B Use divisions to answer these questions:

☆ How many packs of 4 toys can be made from 864 toys?   4⟌8̄6̄4̄ (216)

1 How many boxes holding 6 eggs each can be filled with 672 eggs?

2 How many cars can each be fitted with 4 wheels if there are 456 wheels altogether?

3 How many boxes holding 8 plants can be made up if there are 896 plants altogether?

4 How many £5 notes have the same value as £580?

D Answer these questions:

☆ 5 equal tanks can be filled with 605 litres of water. How much does each tank hold?   5⟌6̄0̄5̄ (121)

1 2 equal tanks can be filled with 948 litres of petrol. How much does each tank hold?

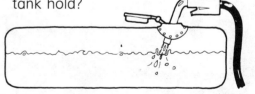

2 968 potatoes are planted in 8 equal rows. How many potatoes in each row?

3 Share 486 grapes equally among 3 gorillas. How many grapes each?

Divide 744 by 6: $6\overline{)744}$

divide 7 hundreds by 6: $6\overline{)744}$

divide 4 tens by 6: $6\overline{)744}$

divide 4 units by 6: $6\overline{)744}$

744÷6=124

Divide 838 by 3:

$3\overline{)838}$ 279 r1

Divide 624 by 5:

$5\overline{)624}$ 124 r 4

A Copy and complete:

☆ $4\overline{)572}$ $4\overline{)572}$ 143

1 $3\overline{)465}$ 4 $5\overline{)730}$

2 $6\overline{)732}$ 5 $4\overline{)632}$

3 $2\overline{)516}$ 6 $3\overline{)138}$

B How much does each person receive when:

☆ a prize of £532 is shared equally among 4 people? $4\overline{)£532}$ £133

1 a prize of £538 is shared equally between 2 people?

2 a prize of £828 is shared equally among 6 people?

3 a prize of £135 is shared equally among 5 people?

4 a prize of £266 is shared equally among 7 people?

C Copy and complete:

☆ $5\overline{)732}$ $5\overline{)732}$ 146r2

1 $4\overline{)553}$ 5 $3\overline{)223}$

2 $6\overline{)854}$ 6 $5\overline{)214}$

3 $3\overline{)751}$ 7 $2\overline{)557}$

4 $4\overline{)713}$ 8 $8\overline{)427}$

D How many are left over when:

☆ 373 cakes are packed in boxes of 4? $4\overline{)373}$ 93r1

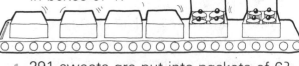

1 291 sweets are put into packets of 6?

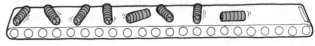

2 353 T-shirts are packed in boxes of 8?

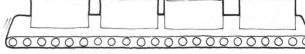

3 795 rubbers are packed in boxes of 4?

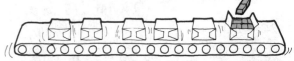

4 653 pencils are packed in boxes of 9?

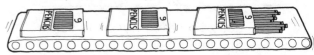

A Write numbers for ✳'s:

1 4×7=✳   6 6×7=✳   11 6×4=✳
2 3×6=✳   7 8×4=✳   12 5×9=✳
3 5×4=✳   8 7×5=✳   13 7×8=✳
4 10×9=✳   9 2×8=✳   14 8×9=✳
5 9×5=✳   10 9×7=✳   15 3×9=✳

B Copy and complete:

    1   2 8 4   3   2 4 8   5   1 6 6
         ×   7   ×   6   ×   8

    2   1 6 9   4   3 9 0   6   2 7 8
         ×   5   ×   5   ×   4

C Answer these questions:

1 There are 125 wafers in each box. How many wafers in 6 boxes?

2 What is the value of ten £20 notes?

3 What is the product of 123 and 4?

4 What is the product of 36 and 10?

5 Circus tickets cost £1·85 each. How much does Mr Jenkins have to pay for 6 tickets?

6 Computers cost £89 each. What is the total cost of 10 computers?

7 Packs of sweets cost 67p each. What is the total cost of 9 packs?

8 Mrs Williams' train fare is £2·65. How much does she pay for 8 journeys?

9 Glasses hold 232 millilitres each. What is the total capacity of 4 glasses?

10 What is the product of 235 and 10?

D Write the **factors** of:

1 15   4 18   7 35
2 16   5 24   8 48
3 28   6 21   9 64

E Write numbers for ✳'s:

1 15÷5=✳   7 54÷9=✳
2 24÷3=✳   8 270÷10=✳
3 35÷7=✳   9 56÷8=✳
4 60÷10=✳   10 81÷9=✳
5 36÷4=✳   11 72÷8=✳
6 130÷10=✳   12 3250÷10=✳

F Copy and complete:

1 6)342   3 3)628   5 6)803
2 5)890   4 4)727   6 9)426

G Answer these questions:

1 8 people are given an equal share of £272. How much does each person receive?

2 $\frac{1}{2}$ of the children at St James School are girls. If there are 364 children, how many girls are there?

3 Eight litres of Fizzo cost £5·68. What is the cost of 1 litre?

4 435 flowers are planted in 5 equal rows. How many flowers in each row?

5 4 barrels hold 1940 litres. How much does one barrel hold if they each have the same capacity?

6 Rolls are sold in packs of eight. How many packs can be made with 392 rolls?

A Copy and complete this giant multiplication square on squared paper.

Use a calculator only when you need to.

Your multiplication square can help you to find **factors**.

How many different **factors** can you find for each of the numbers from 1 to 16?

Record your results in a table.

Which numbers in your table have an odd number of factors?

Write down the first four square numbers.

Compare this answer with your last answer. What do you find?

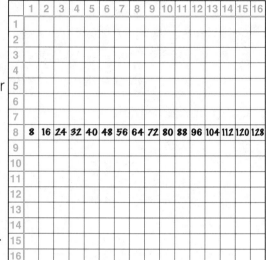

	1	2	3	4	5	6	7	8	9	10	11	12	13	14	15	16
1																
2																
3																
4																
5																
6																
7																
8	8	16	24	32	40	48	56	64	72	80	88	96	104	112	120	128
9																
10																
11																
12																
13																
14																
15																
16																

Find 5 larger numbers that have an odd number of factors.

B The **digital sum** for the number 35 is **8** $3 + 5 = 8$

The digital sum for the number 76 is **4**. $7 + 6 = 13$
$$1 + 3 = 4$$

On a sheet of squared paper rewrite the giant multiplication square from the last investigation but replace each of the numbers by its digital sum.

Describe any patterns you can find on your new square.

This drawing has been made starting at point A and using the first eleven numbers on the 8th line of your square.

Explain how the drawing has been created.

Copy and continue the drawing on squared paper.

Make some more patterns like these using other lines of numbers from your square.

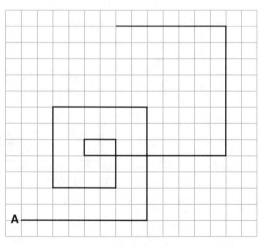

Answer any questions you can. Leave those you cannot do.
You should not use a calculator for the questions on this page.

Copy and complete these multiplication squares:

1
×	6	8	4
5			
7			
9			

2
×	3	7	9
6			
8			
9			

Copy and complete:

3
```
   2 1 6
 ×     4
```

4
```
   1 5 4
 ×     4
```

5
```
   1 6 4
 ×     5
```

6
```
   2 4 6
 ×     7
```

7
```
   4 2 9
 ×     6
```

8 If there are 65 newspapers in a pack, how many newspapers will there be in 6 packs?

9 126 screws are needed to build a cupboard. How many screws will be needed for 8 cupboards?

Write numbers for ∗'s

10 $7 \times 10 = *$

11 $13 \times 10 = *$

12 $78 \times 10 = *$

13 $132 \times 10 = *$

What are the factors of:

14 28? 16 32?

15 16? 17 40?

What is the product of:

18 6 and 5?

19 7 and 9?

20 26 and 4?

21 What is the next square number after 16?

22 What is the next square number after 36?

23 What is the next prime number after 11?

24 What is the next prime number after 23?

Copy and complete the following. Some of your answers will have a remainder.

25 4)808

26 6)607

27 8)848

28 3)561

29 9)478

Write numbers for ∗'s

30 $320 \div 10 = *$

31 $840 \div 10 = *$

32 $1630 \div 10 = *$

33 If eight people have an equal share of £944, how much does each person receive?

34 Use a calculator to work out how many 250 ml cartons can be filled with 263 500 ml of yoghurt.

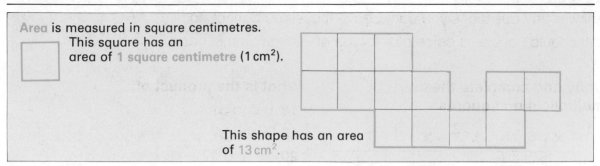

Area is measured in square centimetres.
This square has an
area of **1 square centimetre** (1 cm²).

This shape has an area
of 13 cm².

A What is the **area** of each shape
below?

☆

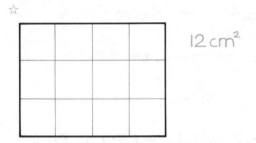

12 cm²

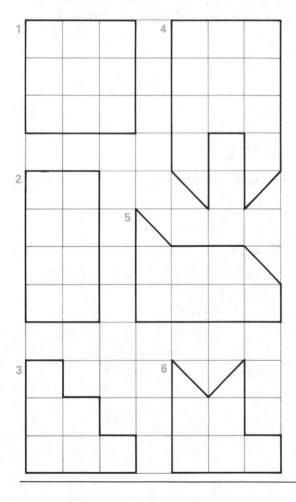

B You need some centimetre squared
paper. Draw a shape that has an
area of:

☆ 8 cm²

1 10 cm²	4 12 cm²	7 $17\frac{1}{2}$ cm²
2 15 cm²	5 14 cm²	8 $19\frac{1}{2}$ cm²
3 9 cm²	6 20 cm²	9 $22\frac{1}{2}$ cm²

C You need some centimetre squared
paper. Draw:

☆ a square that has an
area of 9 cm²

1 a rectangle that has
an area of 24 cm²

2 a square that has an area of 25 cm²

D Which 3 shapes below have the
same **area**?

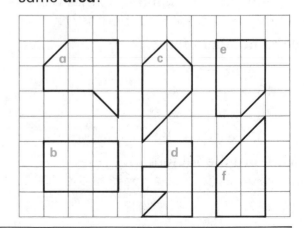

Area

To find the approximate area of this shape:

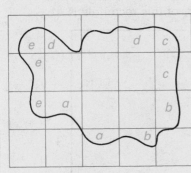

First: Count the whole squares ...   ... whole squares 5cm²
Then: Find parts of squares $a+a=$ *about* 1cm²
       that together have $b+b=$ *about* 1cm²
       about the same area as $c+c=$ *about* 1cm²
       one whole square ... $d+d=$ *about* 1cm²
                                         $e+e+e=$ *about* 1cm²
Then: Find the area left ...   area left= *about* $\frac{1}{2}$cm²
                                         $\overline{10\frac{1}{2}\text{cm}^2}$

So: The area of the shape is **approximately** $10\frac{1}{2}$cm²

A Find the **approximate** area of these shapes:

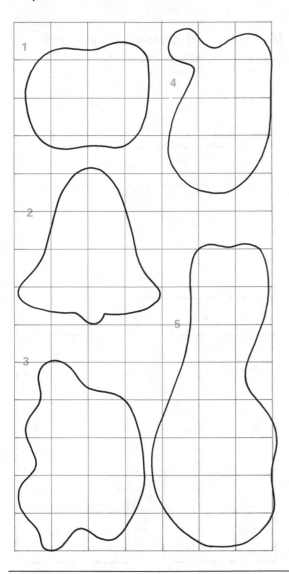

B 1 Estimate the approximate area of this shape.

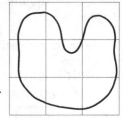

   2 Work out the **approximate** area.

   3 What is the **difference** between your estimate and your answer to question 2?

C Which shape below has:

   1 the smallest area?

   2 the largest area?

   3 an area of approximately 10 cm²?

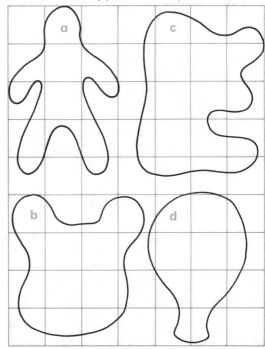

You can use **multiplication**
to find the **area** of this rectangle:

There are 5 squares in each row.
There are 3 rows.
5×3=15
The area of this rectangle is 15 cm²

The length of this rectangle is 5 cm.
The breadth of this rectangle is 4 cm.

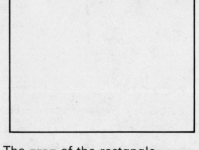

The area of the rectangle
can be found by multiplication:
5 × 4 = 20. The area is 20 cm²

A Use **multiplication** to find the areas
of these rectangles:

☆

6 cm²

1

2

3

4

5

B Measure and **multiply** to find the
areas of these rectangles:

☆

6 x 2 = 12   area 12 cm²

1

3

2

4

Area

A Answer these questions:

1 What is the area of the rectangle:

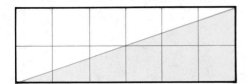

2 What is the name of the **orange** line?

3 What fraction of the rectangle is shaded?

4 What is the area of the shaded part?

B What is the area of each rectangle? What is the area of each shaded triangle?

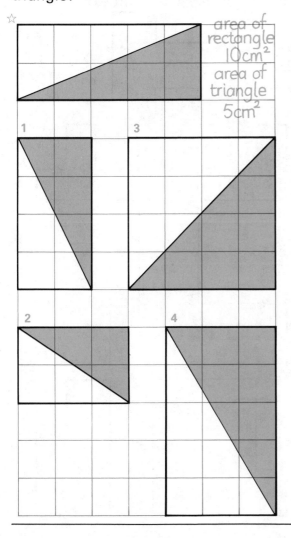

area of rectangle 10cm²

area of triangle 5cm²

What is the area of this triangle?

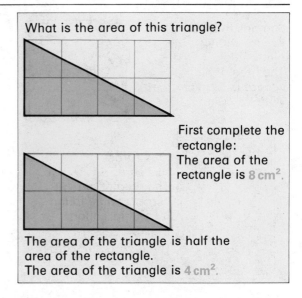

First complete the rectangle:
The area of the rectangle is 8 cm².

The area of the triangle is half the area of the rectangle.
The area of the triangle is 4 cm².

C Work out the area of each triangle below:

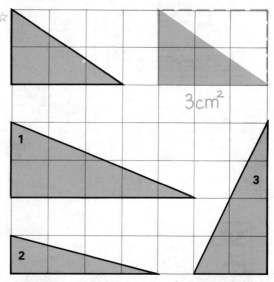

3cm²

D Work out the area of the shaded triangle:

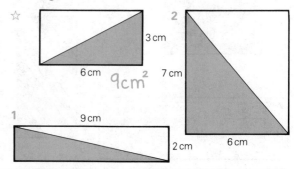

9cm²

Ben has made a
square with 4
metre rules.
The area of his
square is **1 square metre.**
Write: **1 m²**

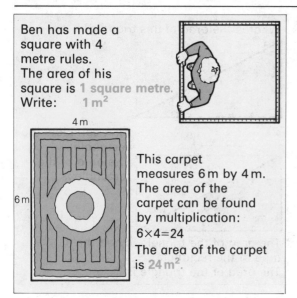

4 m

6 m

This carpet
measures 6 m by 4 m.
The area of the
carpet can be found
by multiplication:
$6 \times 4 = 24$
The area of the carpet
is **24 m².**

To measure the area of this floor,
divide the shape into 2 rectangles:

10 m

4 m

3 m

4 m

Use multiplication to find the area of each
rectangle: **10×4=40**   **4×3=12**
Total area of floor=40 m²+12 m²=**52 m².**

A Work out the area of these carpets:

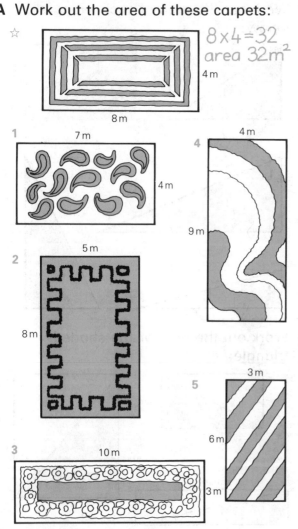

☆

$8 \times 4 = 32$
area 32 m²

4 m

8 m

1

7 m

4 m

4

4 m

4 m

9 m

2

5 m

8 m

5

3 m

6 m

3 m

3

10 m

B Work out these floor areas:

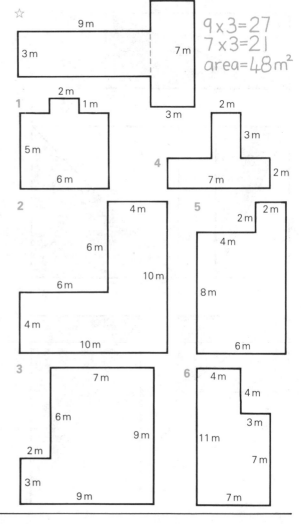

☆

9 m

3 m

7 m

$9 \times 3 = 27$
$7 \times 3 = 21$
area = 48 m²

3 m

1

2 m

1 m

5 m

6 m

4

2 m

3 m

7 m

2 m

2

4 m

6 m

6 m

10 m

4 m

10 m

5

2 m

2 m

4 m

8 m

6 m

3

7 m

6 m

9 m

2 m

3 m

9 m

6

4 m

4 m

3 m

11 m

7 m

7 m

Area

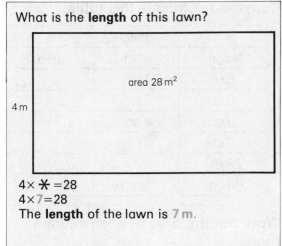

What is the **length** of this lawn?

area 28 m²

4 m

4× ✳ =28
4×7=28
The **length** of the lawn is 7 m.

What is the **width** of this swimming pool?

area
96 m²

12 m

12× ✳ =96
12×8=96
The **width** is 8 m.

A Work out the **lengths** of these lawns:

☆
7 m

area
56 m²

7x✳=56
7x8=56
length=8m

1
6 m
area
54 m²

4
5 m
area
35 m²

2
6 m
area
42 m²

5
3 m
area
24 m²

3
5 m
area
50 m²

6
8 m
area
72 m²

B Work out the **widths** of these
swimming pools:

☆
10 m
area
60 m²

10x✳=60
10x6=60
Width=6m

3
9 m
area
54 m²

1
9 m
area
27 m²

4
5 m
area
20 m²

2
8 m
area
48 m²

5
10 m
area
70 m²

C Copy and complete:

	length of rectangle	width of rectangle	area of rectangle
☆	6 m	5 m	30 m²
1	4 m	9 m	
2	5 m		50 m²
3		8 m	64 m²
4		6 m	30 m²
5	9 m		72 m²

Revision for pages 48–53

A Which 3 shapes below have the same area?

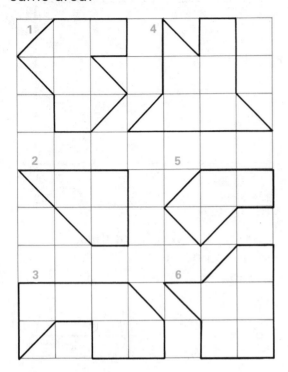

B Work out the approximate area of these shapes:

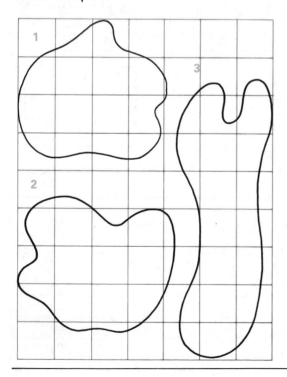

C Copy and complete this table:

	rectangles		
	length	width	area
1	6 m	4 m	
2	5 cm	7 cm	
3	9 cm	8 cm	
4	10 cm	6 cm	
5	28 m	6 m	
6	64 cm	8 cm	

D Work out the area of each shaded triangle:

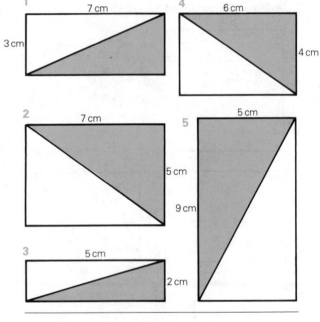

E Work out these floor areas:

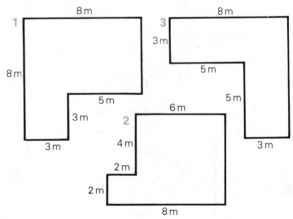

A Farmers keep sheep in pens. On centimetre squared paper, draw designs for 8 different shaped sheep pens. Each design should enclose an area of 20 cm².

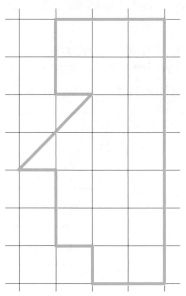

If the side of each square on your designs represents a length of 1 metre, work out the approximate length of fencing that would be needed for each of your pens.

For example, this pen would need approximately 23 m of fencing.

Label your pen designs A, B, C, D, E, F, G and H. Which of your pens would need the longest length of fencing to build?

Design 10 different pens each of which can be built using 20 m of fencing. Which of your pens encloses:
a) the greatest area? b) the smallest area?

B Work out the floor area of your classroom as accurately as you can.

Work out the cost of fitting a carpet in your classroom.

You can choose a carpet from a catalogue or choose one of the carpets here:

When you work out the cost of fitting the carpet, allow an extra 2 m² of carpet for pieces that are wasted when it is cut into shape.

Allow $\frac{1}{10}$ of the total cost of the carpet to pay the carpet fitters.

Costs are per square metre

£4.50 £4.80

£5.20 £6.50

C Work out the approximate area that your hand covers when you place it on a flat surface.

Work out the area that your foot covers when you place it on a flat surface.

Do you think that people with larger hands also have larger feet?

Investigate this by measuring the areas covered by the hands and feet of a least 8 other children in your class.

Work out the approximate area of skin that is needed to cover one of your hands up to your wrist.

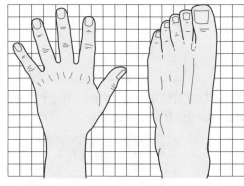

Answer any questions you can. Leave those you cannot do.

The shapes below are drawn on centimetre squared paper.

What is the area of each shape?

1

2

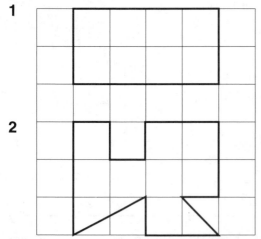

7

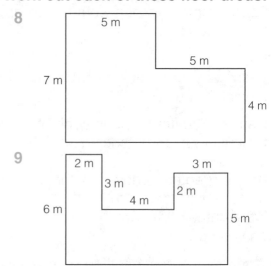

3 cm

7 cm

Work out each of these floor areas:

8

5 m

5 m

7 m

4 m

9

2 m

3 m

3 m

6 m

4 m

2 m

3 m

5 m

What is the approximate area of this shape?

3

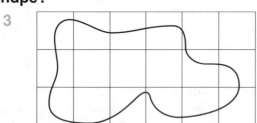

Work out the lengths of each of these carpets:

10

area 48 m²

4 m

What is the area of each of these rectangles?

4

6 cm

3 cm

5

11 cm

3 cm

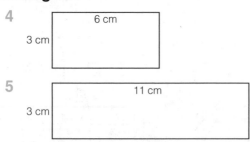

11

area 48 m²

6 m

Work out the area of this lawn:

What is the area of each of these coloured triangles?

6

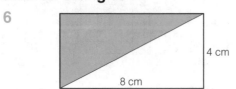

8 cm

4 cm

12

57 m

28 m

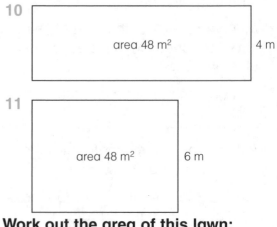

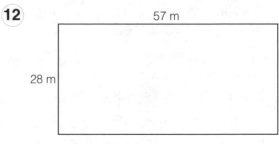

Crash landing

A Write the answers to each of these questions:

☆ $54 \div 9 =$ ✳   6

1 $48 \div 6 =$ ✳   9 $13 \times 5 =$ ✳
2 $9 \times 3 =$ ✳   10 $11 \times 6 =$ ✳
3 $4 \times 7 =$ ✳   11 $27 + 24 + 20 =$ ✳
4 $6 \times 6 =$ ✳   12 $8 \times 9 =$ ✳
5 $13 \times 3 =$ ✳   13 $132 - 49 =$ ✳
6 $96 - 49 =$ ✳   14 $12 \times 7 =$ ✳
7 $7 \times 7 =$ ✳   15 $17 \times 5 =$ ✳
8 $8 \times 8 =$ ✳

B Find each of your answers from **A** in one of the squares below. Write down the letters in each square to find a **hidden message**:

☆ $54 \div 9 = $**6**   **Write:**   DI

1	2	3	4	5	6	7	8	9	10
TH	E	PL	AN	E	DI	VE	D	OU	T
11	12	13	14	15	16	17	18	19	20
OF		CON	TR	OL	...	T	HE		RA	DI	O
21	22	23	24	25	26	27	28	29	30
CR	AC	KL	ED		......		YO	U	MU	ST
31	32	33	34	35	36	37	38	39	40
ST	AR	T	TH	E	EN	GI	NE	J	OE,
41	42	43	44	45	46	47	48	49	50
TH	ER	E	CA	N	BE	O	NL	Y	
51	52	53	54	55	56	57	58	59	60
TW	EN	TY	S	EC	ON	DS		LE	F	T
61	62	63	64	65	66	67	68	69	70
BE	FO	RE		YO	U	R	PL	AN	E	
71	72	73	74	75	76	77	78	79	80
BR	EA	KS		U	P.	TH	E	LE	VE	R'S
81	82	83	84	85	86	87	88	89	90
ST	UC	K	FA	ST		Y	EL	LE	D	
91	92	93	94	95	96	97	98	99	100
JO	E.	I'M		G	OI	NG		TO		JU	MP

Where did Joe land?

You need a hundred square.

1	2	3	4	5	6	7	8	9	10
11	12	13	14	15	16	17	18	19	20
21	22	23	24	25	26	27	28	29	30
31	32	33	34	35	36	37	38	39	40
41	42	43	44	45	46	47	48	49	50
51	52	53	54	55	56	57	58	59	60
61	62	63	64	65	66	67	68	69	70
71	72	73	74	75	76	77	78	79	80
81	82	83	84	85	86	87	88	89	90
91	92	93	94	95	96	97	98	99	100

C On your hundred square, shade all the answers to these questions:

☆ $24 + 28 =$ ✳   52

1 $5 \times 6 =$ ✳   22 $12 \times 7 =$ ✳
2 $84 - 71 =$ ✳   23 $44 + 38 =$ ✳
3 $88 \div 8 =$ ✳   24 $147 \div 7 =$ ✳
4 $28 + 38 =$ ✳   25 $33 + 65 =$ ✳
5 $4 \times 7 =$ ✳   26 $8 \times 8 =$ ✳
6 $80 - 49 =$ ✳   27 $200 - 103 =$ ✳
7 $64 \div 8 =$ ✳   28 $100 - 59 =$ ✳
8 $49 + 25 =$ ✳   29 $6 \times 9 =$ ✳
9 $5 \times 8 =$ ✳   30 $12 \times 8 =$ ✳
10 $100 - 8 =$ ✳   31 $100 \div 10 =$ ✳
11 $24 \div 8 =$ ✳   32 $145 - 122 =$ ✳
12 $18 + 75 =$ ✳   33 $11 \times 2 =$ ✳
13 $11 \times 9 =$ ✳   34 $7 \times 8 =$ ✳
14 $46 + 48 =$ ✳   35 $65 - 27 =$ ✳
15 $120 \div 6 =$ ✳   36 $16 \div 8 =$ ✳
16 $19 + 67 =$ ✳   37 $9 \times 8 =$ ✳
17 $5 \times 10 =$ ✳   38 $81 - 28 =$ ✳
18 $10 \div 10 =$ ✳   39 $54 \div 3 =$ ✳
19 $27 \div 3 =$ ✳   40 $29 + 47 =$ ✳
20 $124 - 62 =$ ✳   41 $7 \times 7 =$ ✳
21 $6 \times 8 =$ ✳

A What **fraction** of each shape has been shaded?

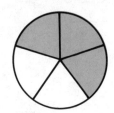

$\frac{3}{5}$

1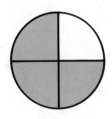

3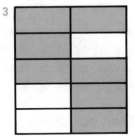

2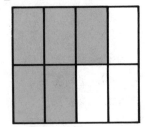

4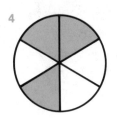

B Copy and complete:

1 whole		
$\frac{1}{3}$	$\frac{1}{3}$	$\frac{1}{3}$

| $\frac{1}{6}$ | $\frac{1}{6}$ | $\frac{1}{6}$ | $\frac{1}{6}$ | $\frac{1}{6}$ | $\frac{1}{6}$ |

☆ $\frac{2}{3} = \frac{*}{6}$

$\frac{2}{3} = \frac{4}{6}$

1 $\frac{1}{3} = \frac{*}{6}$ 3 $\frac{4}{6} = \frac{*}{3}$

2 $\frac{3}{3} = \frac{*}{6}$ 4 $\frac{3}{6} = \frac{*}{2}$

C Copy and complete:

1 whole				
$\frac{1}{5}$	$\frac{1}{5}$	$\frac{1}{5}$	$\frac{1}{5}$	$\frac{1}{5}$

| $\frac{1}{10}$ | $\frac{1}{10}$ | $\frac{1}{10}$ | $\frac{1}{10}$ | $\frac{1}{10}$ | $\frac{1}{10}$ | $\frac{1}{10}$ | $\frac{1}{10}$ | $\frac{1}{10}$ | $\frac{1}{10}$ |

☆ $\frac{3}{5} = \frac{*}{10}$

$\frac{3}{5} = \frac{6}{10}$

1 $\frac{1}{5} = \frac{*}{10}$ 3 $\frac{6}{10} = \frac{*}{5}$ 5 $\frac{2}{5} = \frac{*}{10}$

2 $\frac{4}{5} = \frac{*}{10}$ 4 $\frac{5}{5} = \frac{*}{10}$ 6 $\frac{5}{10} = \frac{*}{2}$

D Draw these shapes on squared paper. Colour the fraction shown:

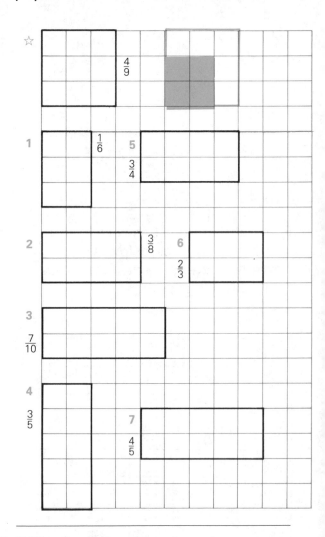

E Write these fractions in order, **smallest first**:

☆ $\frac{1}{2}$ $\frac{1}{4}$ $\frac{1}{3}$ $\frac{1}{8}$

$\frac{1}{8}$ $\frac{1}{4}$ $\frac{1}{3}$ $\frac{1}{2}$

1 $\frac{4}{5}$ $\frac{3}{5}$ $\frac{1}{5}$ $\frac{2}{5}$

2 $\frac{7}{8}$ $\frac{3}{8}$ $\frac{1}{8}$ $\frac{5}{8}$

3 $\frac{3}{10}$ $\frac{2}{5}$ $\frac{7}{10}$ $\frac{4}{5}$

4 $\frac{2}{3}$ $\frac{5}{6}$ $\frac{1}{3}$ $\frac{1}{6}$

5 $\frac{3}{4}$ $\frac{1}{8}$ $\frac{2}{2}$ $\frac{5}{8}$ $\frac{1}{2}$

Fractions

A Copy the fractions on these number lines.
Write fractions for ✳'s:

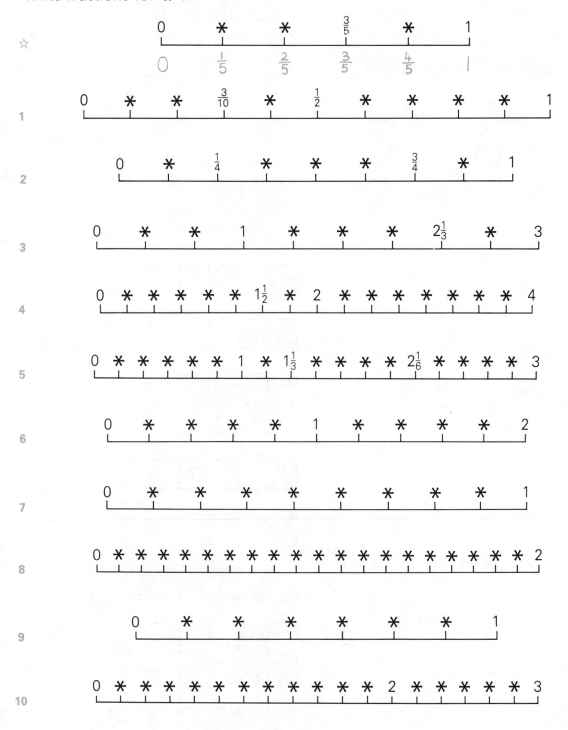

1 whole											
$\frac{1}{2}$						$\frac{1}{2}$					
$\frac{1}{3}$				$\frac{1}{3}$				$\frac{1}{3}$			
$\frac{1}{4}$			$\frac{1}{4}$			$\frac{1}{4}$			$\frac{1}{4}$		
$\frac{1}{5}$		$\frac{1}{5}$		$\frac{1}{5}$		$\frac{1}{5}$		$\frac{1}{5}$			
$\frac{1}{6}$		$\frac{1}{6}$		$\frac{1}{6}$		$\frac{1}{6}$		$\frac{1}{6}$		$\frac{1}{6}$	
$\frac{1}{7}$	$\frac{1}{7}$	$\frac{1}{7}$	$\frac{1}{7}$	$\frac{1}{7}$	$\frac{1}{7}$	$\frac{1}{7}$					
$\frac{1}{8}$	$\frac{1}{8}$	$\frac{1}{8}$	$\frac{1}{8}$	$\frac{1}{8}$	$\frac{1}{8}$	$\frac{1}{8}$	$\frac{1}{8}$				
$\frac{1}{9}$	$\frac{1}{9}$	$\frac{1}{9}$	$\frac{1}{9}$	$\frac{1}{9}$	$\frac{1}{9}$	$\frac{1}{9}$	$\frac{1}{9}$	$\frac{1}{9}$			
$\frac{1}{10}$	$\frac{1}{10}$	$\frac{1}{10}$	$\frac{1}{10}$	$\frac{1}{10}$	$\frac{1}{10}$	$\frac{1}{10}$	$\frac{1}{10}$	$\frac{1}{10}$	$\frac{1}{10}$		
$\frac{1}{12}$	$\frac{1}{12}$	$\frac{1}{12}$	$\frac{1}{12}$	$\frac{1}{12}$	$\frac{1}{12}$	$\frac{1}{12}$	$\frac{1}{12}$	$\frac{1}{12}$	$\frac{1}{12}$	$\frac{1}{12}$	$\frac{1}{12}$

A Use the diagram to help you.
Write numbers for ✶'s:

☆ $\frac{1}{3} = \frac{✶}{6} = \frac{✶}{9} = \frac{✶}{12}$

$\frac{1}{3} = \frac{2}{6} = \frac{3}{9} = \frac{4}{12}$

1 $\frac{1}{2} = \frac{✶}{4} = \frac{✶}{8} = \frac{✶}{12}$

2 $\frac{2}{3} = \frac{✶}{6} = \frac{✶}{9} = \frac{✶}{12}$

3 $\frac{1}{2} = \frac{✶}{10}$

4 $\frac{1}{2} = \frac{✶}{6} = \frac{✶}{8} = \frac{✶}{10}$

5 $\frac{3}{4} = \frac{✶}{8} = \frac{✶}{12}$

6 $\frac{5}{6} = \frac{✶}{12}$

7 1 whole $= \frac{✶}{2} = \frac{✶}{5} = \frac{✶}{7} = \frac{✶}{9}$

B Write the sign < or > for ✶'s:

☆ $\frac{4}{10} ✶ \frac{1}{2}$ <   5 $\frac{3}{5} ✶ \frac{7}{10}$

1 $\frac{1}{2} ✶ \frac{3}{4}$ 6 $\frac{4}{12} ✶ \frac{1}{4}$

2 $\frac{1}{4} ✶ \frac{3}{8}$ 7 $\frac{3}{4} ✶ \frac{5}{8}$

3 $\frac{5}{6} ✶ \frac{2}{3}$ 8 $\frac{5}{10} ✶ \frac{3}{5}$

4 $\frac{3}{8} ✶ \frac{1}{2}$

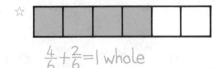

$\frac{5}{8}$ of this shape is shaded.

$\frac{3}{8}$ of the shape is unshaded.

$\frac{5}{8} + \frac{3}{8} = 1$ whole.

C Write sums for each of these:

☆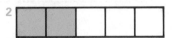

$\frac{4}{6} + \frac{2}{6} = 1$ whole

1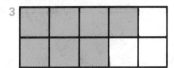

2

3

4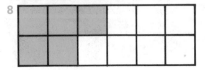

5

6

7

8

Fractions

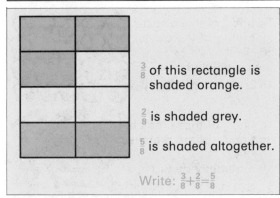

$\frac{3}{8}$ of this rectangle is shaded orange.

$\frac{2}{8}$ is shaded grey.

$\frac{5}{8}$ is shaded altogether.

Write: $\frac{3}{8} + \frac{2}{8} = \frac{5}{8}$

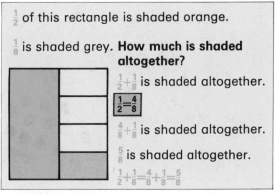

$\frac{1}{2}$ of this rectangle is shaded orange.

$\frac{1}{8}$ is shaded grey. **How much is shaded altogether?**

$\frac{1}{2} + \frac{1}{8}$ is shaded altogether.

$\boxed{\frac{1}{2} = \frac{4}{8}}$

$\frac{4}{8} + \frac{1}{8}$ is shaded altogether.

$\frac{5}{8}$ is shaded altogether.

$\frac{1}{2} + \frac{1}{8} = \frac{4}{8} + \frac{1}{8} = \frac{5}{8}$

A Write sums for these:

B Work out how much of each shape is shaded altogether. Copy and complete:

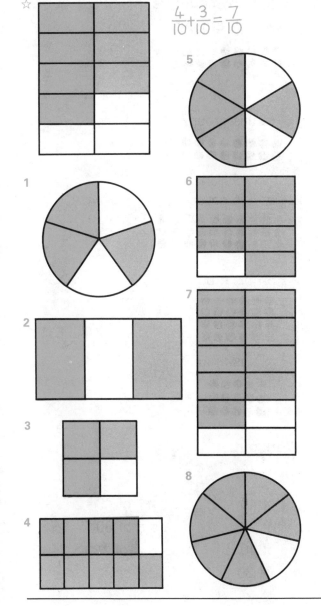

$\frac{4}{10} + \frac{3}{10} = \frac{7}{10}$

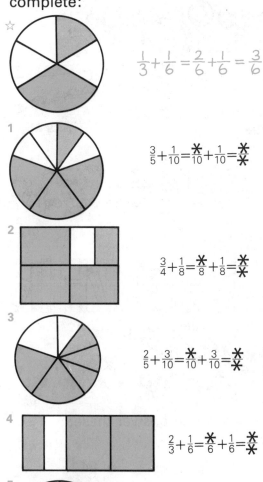

$\frac{1}{3} + \frac{1}{6} = \frac{2}{6} + \frac{1}{6} = \frac{3}{6}$

1    $\frac{3}{5} + \frac{1}{10} = \frac{*}{10} + \frac{1}{10} = \frac{*}{*}$

2    $\frac{3}{4} + \frac{1}{8} = \frac{*}{8} + \frac{1}{8} = \frac{*}{*}$

3    $\frac{2}{5} + \frac{3}{10} = \frac{*}{10} + \frac{3}{10} = \frac{*}{*}$

4    $\frac{2}{3} + \frac{1}{6} = \frac{*}{6} + \frac{1}{6} = \frac{*}{*}$

5    $\frac{1}{5} + \frac{7}{10} = \frac{*}{10} + \frac{7}{10} = \frac{*}{*}$

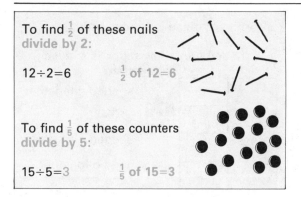

To find $\frac{1}{2}$ of these nails
divide by 2:

$12 \div 2 = 6$ $\frac{1}{2}$ of $12 = 6$

To find $\frac{1}{5}$ of these counters
divide by 5:

$15 \div 5 = 3$ $\frac{1}{5}$ of $15 = 3$

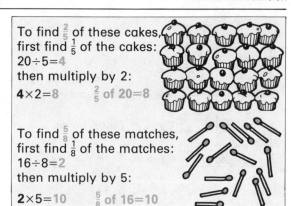

To find $\frac{2}{5}$ of these cakes,
first find $\frac{1}{5}$ of the cakes:
$20 \div 5 = 4$
then multiply by 2:
$4 \times 2 = 8$ $\frac{2}{5}$ of $20 = 8$

To find $\frac{5}{8}$ of these matches,
first find $\frac{1}{8}$ of the matches:
$16 \div 8 = 2$
then multiply by 5:
$2 \times 5 = 10$ $\frac{5}{8}$ of $16 = 10$

A Use division to answer these:

☆ $\frac{1}{3}$ of 18 marbles

$18 \div 3 = 6$

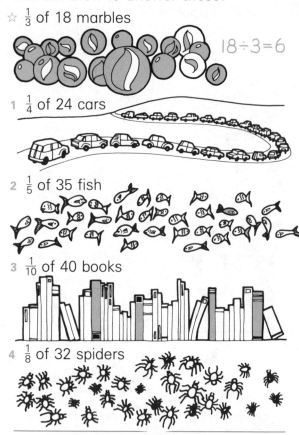

1 $\frac{1}{4}$ of 24 cars

2 $\frac{1}{5}$ of 35 fish

3 $\frac{1}{10}$ of 40 books

4 $\frac{1}{8}$ of 32 spiders

B Use division to answer these:

☆ $\frac{1}{10}$ of 60 $60 \div 10 = 6$

1 $\frac{1}{2}$ of 18   6 $\frac{1}{8}$ of 64

2 $\frac{1}{3}$ of 24   7 $\frac{1}{4}$ of 40

3 $\frac{1}{5}$ of 40   8 $\frac{1}{7}$ of 42

4 $\frac{1}{6}$ of 36   9 $\frac{1}{9}$ of 72

5 $\frac{1}{10}$ of 90   10 $\frac{1}{5}$ of 60

C How many counters in:

☆ $\frac{3}{10}$ of this group?

$20 \div 10 = 2$
$2 \times 3 = 6$

1 $\frac{3}{4}$ of this group?

2 $\frac{5}{6}$ of this group?

3 $\frac{7}{8}$ of this group?

4 $\frac{4}{5}$ of this group?

D Work out:

☆ $\frac{5}{6}$ of 24 $24 \div 6 = 4$
                                      $4 \times 5 = 20$

1 $\frac{3}{5}$ of 40   5 $\frac{4}{5}$ of 45

2 $\frac{2}{3}$ of 27   6 $\frac{3}{4}$ of 80

3 $\frac{3}{8}$ of 40   7 $\frac{3}{10}$ of 100

4 $\frac{7}{10}$ of 30   8 $\frac{7}{9}$ of 81

Mrs Carter has 96p. She gives Alice $\frac{3}{4}$ of the money and the other $\frac{1}{4}$ she gives to John. How much money is given to each child?

$$\begin{array}{r} 24 \\ 4\overline{)9\,6} \end{array}$$

$\frac{1}{4}$ of 96p is **24p**

John is given 24p.

$$\begin{array}{r} 2\,4 \\ \times\ 3 \\ \hline 72 \\ \scriptstyle 1 \end{array}$$

$\frac{3}{4}$ of 96p is **72p**

Alice is given 72p.

A Now answer these:

☆ A hockey team scored 48 goals during the season. Mary scored $\frac{3}{8}$ of the goals. How many goals did she score?

$\frac{1}{8}$ of 48 = 6. $\frac{3}{8}$ of 48 = 18 goals

1 A piece of string is 155 cm long. $\frac{3}{5}$ of the string is used to tie a parcel. How much string is used?

2 Mr Fixit has 172 nails. He uses $\frac{3}{4}$ of these to make a box. How many nails does he use?

3 $\frac{5}{6}$ of the days in June were sunny. How many days were sunny?

4 Buster weighed 72 kg. After a diet he had lost $\frac{1}{8}$ of this weight. How much weight did he lose?

5 Mike had £36. He spent $\frac{3}{4}$ of this on a radio. How much had he left?

6 A watering can holds 14 litres. If $\frac{3}{7}$ of the water is used, how much water is left?

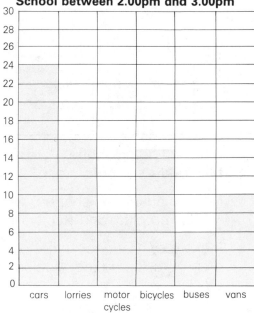

Traffic passing Hill End School between 2.00pm and 3.00pm

(bar graph with vertical axis marked 0, 2, 4, 6, 8, 10, 12, 14, 16, 18, 20, 22, 24, 26, 28, 30 and horizontal axis labelled: cars, lorries, motor cycles, bicycles, buses, vans)

B Use the graph to answer these questions:

☆ $\frac{3}{8}$ of the cars were red. How many cars were red?

$\frac{1}{8}$ of 24 = 3
$\frac{3}{8}$ of 24 = 9

1 $\frac{1}{2}$ of the buses were full. How many buses were full?

2 $\frac{1}{4}$ of the lorries were travelling West. How many lorries were travelling West?

3 $\frac{3}{5}$ of the vans belonged to Bloggs the Builder. How many vans belonged to Bloggs?

4 $\frac{3}{4}$ of the motor cycle riders were learners. How many were **not** learners?

5 $\frac{2}{5}$ of the bicycles were ridden by ladies. How many lady cyclists were there?

6 $\frac{5}{6}$ of the cars were travelling East. How many cars were travelling East?

A Copy each of these rectangles on centimetre squared paper.

Make a flag on shape A with $\frac{1}{6}$ coloured red, $\frac{1}{3}$ coloured blue and $\frac{1}{2}$ coloured green.

Make a pattern on shape B with $\frac{5}{12}$ coloured yellow, $\frac{1}{3}$ coloured blue, and $\frac{1}{4}$ coloured black.

Make a symmetrical shape on shape C with $\frac{3}{8}$ coloured green, $\frac{1}{4}$ coloured red, $\frac{1}{8}$ coloured blue and $\frac{1}{4}$ coloured black.

Design a flag so that $\frac{3}{10}$ of it is coloured in your favourite colour.

B Copy the table below.

Estimate the fraction you think you will find in each survey. Write your estimates in the table.

Carry out each survey and write your results in the table.

For each survey say if the fraction you estimated was too high or too low.

For surveys 2 and 3 choose all of the children before you begin the survey.

Survey. What fraction of:	I estimate the fraction will be	The fraction was	My estimate was (too high / too low)
The first 10 letters in my reading book are vowels			
12 children in the class have a bigger span than me			
10 children in the class have a brother			

Repeat these investigations using larger groups. For example: study 100 letters for survey 1.

How do the fractions change in the larger surveys?

Answer any questions you can. Leave those you cannot do.

Write down the largest fraction in each group.

1 $\frac{1}{3}$ $\frac{1}{2}$ $\frac{1}{4}$ $\frac{1}{8}$ $\frac{1}{6}$

2 $\frac{1}{10}$ $\frac{1}{4}$ $\frac{1}{12}$ $\frac{1}{5}$ $\frac{1}{8}$

3 $\frac{2}{3}$ $\frac{1}{2}$ $\frac{5}{6}$ $\frac{1}{4}$ $\frac{7}{12}$

4 $\frac{3}{4}$ $\frac{3}{8}$ $\frac{3}{5}$ $\frac{7}{8}$ $\frac{7}{10}$

5 How many tenths are equal to one fifth?

6 How many eighths are equal to three quarters?

7 How many twelfths are equal to one whole?

Write the sign '<' or '>' for ✳'s

8 $\frac{2}{3}$ ✳ $\frac{2}{5}$ 10 $\frac{3}{5}$ ✳ $\frac{7}{10}$

9 $\frac{7}{8}$ ✳ $\frac{3}{4}$ 11 $\frac{11}{12}$ ✳ $\frac{5}{6}$

Write numbers for *'s

12 $\frac{2}{3} = \frac{4}{✳}$ 14 $\frac{✳}{10} = \frac{4}{5}$

13 $\frac{5}{✳} = \frac{1}{2}$ 15 $\frac{✳}{8} = \frac{9}{12}$

For each of the following write the fraction of the shape that is shaded:
a) orange   b) grey
c) either orange or grey

16

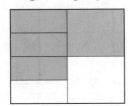

17

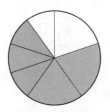

18

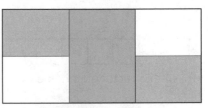

19

What number is:

20 $\frac{1}{10}$ of 30?

21 $\frac{1}{3}$ of 27?

22 $\frac{2}{5}$ of 15?

23 $\frac{3}{4}$ of 32?

24 $\frac{5}{12}$ of 60?

25 $\frac{2}{5}$ of a group of twenty sheep are black. How many are not black?

26 Michael is given £24 as a present. If he spends $\frac{5}{8}$ of his money, how much has he left?

27 $\frac{9}{10}$ of a class of 30 children are present. How many are absent?

Write numbers for ✳'s

28 $\frac{3}{4} + \frac{1}{8} = \frac{7}{✳}$

29 $\frac{3}{5} + \frac{3}{10} = \frac{✳}{10}$

30 $\frac{5}{6} - \frac{2}{3} = \frac{✳}{6}$

31 $\frac{1}{2} - \frac{3}{10} = \frac{✳}{10}$

32 $3 = \frac{✳}{5}$

33 $2\frac{1}{4} = \frac{✳}{4}$

34 $\frac{15}{40} = \frac{3}{✳}$

35 $\frac{28}{49} = \frac{✳}{7}$

36 $7\frac{1}{8} = \frac{✳}{8}$

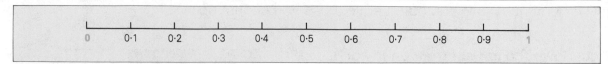

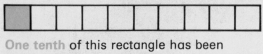

One tenth of this rectangle has been shaded.

We can show this as a **fraction:** $\frac{1}{10}$

or as a **decimal** by using a **decimal point:**

Write: **0·1**
Say: 'nought point one'

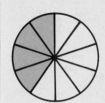

The shaded part of this circle is $\frac{4}{10}$ or **0·4**
Say: 'nought point four'

A Show the shaded part of these shapes as a **fraction** and as a **decimal**:

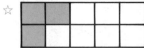

☆ $\frac{3}{10}$; 0·3

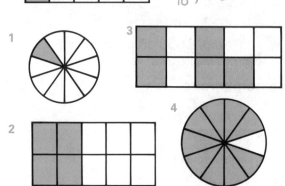

C Copy the shapes below on squared paper. Colour each shape as shown:

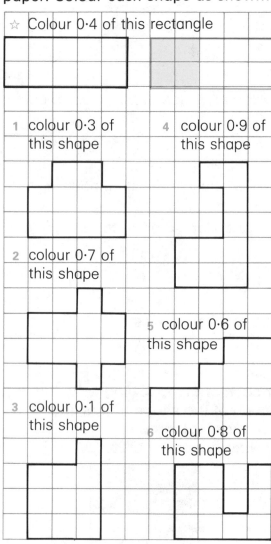

☆ Colour 0·4 of this rectangle

1 colour 0·3 of this shape

4 colour 0·9 of this shape

2 colour 0·7 of this shape

5 colour 0·6 of this shape

3 colour 0·1 of this shape

6 colour 0·8 of this shape

D Write these decimals as **fractions**:

☆ 0·6 $\frac{6}{10}$

1 0·2   5 0·9

2 0·5   6 0·7

3 0·3   7 0·1

4 0·8   8 0·4

B Write these fractions as **decimals**:

☆ $\frac{4}{10}$ 0·4

1 $\frac{2}{10}$ 5 $\frac{3}{10}$

2 $\frac{1}{10}$ 6 $\frac{8}{10}$

3 $\frac{5}{10}$ 7 $\frac{6}{10}$

4 $\frac{7}{10}$ 8 $\frac{9}{10}$

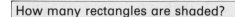

How many rectangles are shaded?

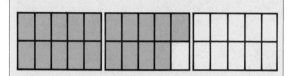

1 whole rectangle is shaded.
$\frac{9}{10}$ of another rectangle is shaded.
Altogether **1·9** rectangles are shaded.
Say: **'one point nine** rectangles are shaded'

A How many rectangles are shaded in each group below?

☆ 1·4

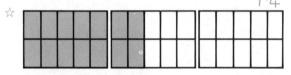

1

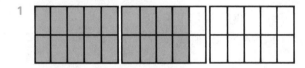

2

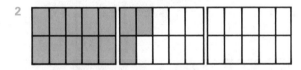

3

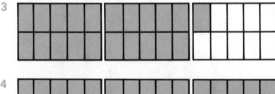

4

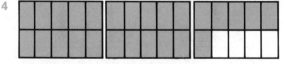

B Write these amounts as decimals:

☆ $2\frac{4}{10}$ 2·4

1 $1\frac{6}{10}$ 3 $2\frac{9}{10}$ 5 $4\frac{8}{10}$

2 $1\frac{3}{10}$ 4 $3\frac{6}{10}$ 6 $9\frac{1}{10}$

---

10 tenths make 1 unit
15 tenths = 1 unit and 5 tenths or 1·5

C How many **tenths** make:

☆ 2 units?   20

1 3 units?   4 7 units?

2 4 units?   5 8 units?

3 5 units?   6 10 units?

D Write these as **decimals**:

☆ 16 tenths   1·6

1 14 tenths   6 29 tenths

2 19 tenths   7 32 tenths

3 18 tenths   8 37 tenths

4 21 tenths   9 46 tenths

5 24 tenths   10 55 tenths

E Write these in order, **smallest first**:

☆ 0·7   1·2   0·5   3·6   0·2

   0·2   0·5   0·7   1·2   3·6

1 0·9   1·5   0·3   1·1   1·6

2 2·3   1·7   0·6   1·6   0·7

3 1·8   2·7   3·6   2·4   0·3

4 3·7   3·1   3·0   6·2   2·6

5 5·2   5·8   6·2   6·8   5·7

6 4·3   3·4   2·3   2·4   4·2

7 6·7   7·6   7·7   6·6   6·8

8 5·2   2·6   6·5   5·6   6·2

9 3·5   8·5   8·3   3·8   5·3

10 7·7   8·8   8·7   7·8   8·0

You can show decimal numbers on an abacus:

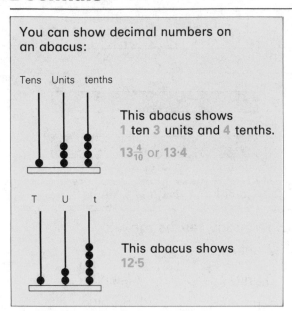

Tens   Units   tenths

This abacus shows
1 ten 3 units and 4 tenths.

$13\frac{4}{10}$ or 13·4

This abacus shows
12·5

A Write the numbers shown on each abacus in **3 different ways**:

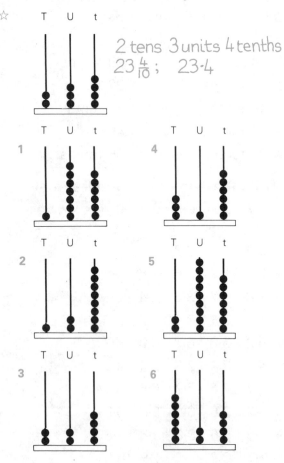

☆   T   U   t

2 tens 3 units 4 tenths
$23\frac{4}{10}$;   23·4

1

2

3

4

5

6

B Draw abacus pictures to show these numbers:

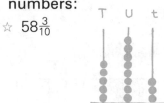

☆ $58\frac{3}{10}$

1	26·2	5	36·4
2	13·9	6	$62\frac{1}{10}$
3	$14\frac{2}{10}$	7	54·7
4	$12\frac{8}{10}$	8	$42\frac{3}{10}$

C Which abacus below shows:

☆ the largest number?   *a*

1 the smallest number?

2 twenty-three and one tenth?

3 $7\frac{9}{10}$?

4 63·3?

5 forty-eight point nine?

6 eighteen point two?

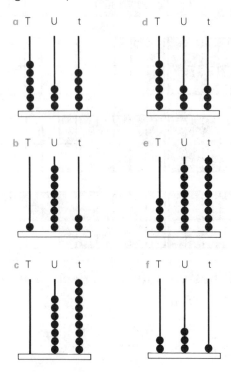

```
0  0·1 0·2 0·3 0·4 0·5 0·6 0·7 0·8 0·9  1  1·1 1·2 1·3 1·4 1·5 1·6 1·7 1·8 1·9  2
```

An elephant drinks
3·5 litres of water and
then another 6·3 litres.
How much water does the
elephant drink altogether?

```
  U t
  3·5 l
+ 6·3 l
  9·8 l    9·8 litres altogether
```

Remember: **10 tenths = 1 unit**
              20 tenths = 2 units
Add together 2·7 and 6·9:

```
  U t
  2·7
+ 6·9
  9·6
  1
```

Add together 16·5, 7·9 and 0·6:

```
  T U t
  1 6·5
    7·9
+   0·6
  2 5·0
  1 2
```

A Copy and complete:

```
☆    U t              U t
     4·2              4·2
  +  3·6           +  3·6
  _____             7·8
```

```
1    U t        3    T U t      5    T U t
     5·3             1 6·2           3 9·2
  +  2·6          + 2 3·6         + 1 6·7
```

```
2    U t        4    T U t      6    T U t
     2·4             2 3·4           3 4·3
  +  5·5          + 2 4·3         + 2 7·5
```

B Answer these questions:

☆ 3 tables measure 2·7 m,
2·8 m and 1·6 m.
What will the total length
be if the tables are
placed end to end?

```
   2·7 m
   2·8 m
+  1·6 m
   7·1 m
```

1 Three buckets hold 3·7 litres, 2·6
litres and 4·6 litres. How much do
they hold altogether?

2 A swimmer swims 28·7 metres, 32·3
metres and then 10·8 metres.
How far does he swim altogether?

C Copy and complete:

```
☆    T U t            T U t
     2 3·7            2 3·7
  + 1 4·8          + 1 4·8
  _____            3 8·5
```

```
1    U t        5    T U t      9    T U t
     3·7             3 3·6           4 6·3
  +  4·6             2 2·9           2 7·7
                  + 1 4·5         + 1 9·4
```

```
2    T U t      6    T U t      10   T U t
     1 5·9           3 5·8           6 3·2
  +  7·8             1 6·7             8·6
                  + 1 9·6         + 2 7·2
```

```
3    T u t      7    T U t      11   T U t
     2 4·7           3 7·5           4 4·1
  + 3 6·8             5·7           3 3·2
                  +   0·8         + 2 2·3
```

```
4    T U t      8    T U t      12   T U t
     2 6·6           2 9·4           7 8·6
  + 3 7·7           2 7·8             0·4
                  +   6·9         + 1 3·2
```

Sally has 1·3 litres of lemonade.
She drinks 0·2 litres.
How much lemonade has she left?

```
  U t
  1·3 l
 −0·2 l      1·1 litres
 ─────       are left.
```

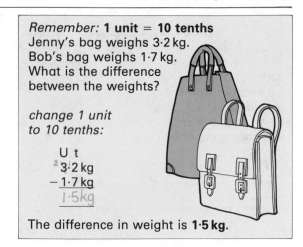

Remember: **1 unit = 10 tenths**
Jenny's bag weighs 3·2 kg.
Bob's bag weighs 1·7 kg.
What is the difference
between the weights?

*change 1 unit
to 10 tenths:*

```
   U t
  ²3·2 kg
 − 1·7 kg
  ────────
   1·5 kg
```

The difference in weight is **1·5 kg**.

A Copy and complete:

```
☆   U t          U t
    2·7          2·7
   −1·4        − 1·4
   ────        ──────
                1·3
```

```
1   U t      3   U t      5   T U t
    3·5          7·9          1 6·8
   −1·3         −3·8        −   4·3
```

```
2   U t      4   U t      6   T U t
    3·8          6·3          2 2·7
   −2·4         −4·0        −1 1·2
```

B Answer these questions:

☆ A piece of string is
6·7 metres long. If
3·4 metres are cut off,
how much is left?

```
  U t
  6·7 m
 −3·4 m
  ──────
  3·3 m
```

1 A sack holds 26·8 kg of flour. If
13·5 kg are taken, how much flour is
left?

2 A barrel holds 86·7 litres
of water. If 32·4 litres are used,
how much water is left?

3 2 boys weigh 62·8 kg and 58·3 kg.
What is the difference between their
weights?

C Copy and complete:

```
☆   T U t         T U t
    1 2·6          1 2·6
   −  3·7        −   3·7
   ──────        ───────
                  8·9
```

```
1   T U t     4   T U t     7   T U t
    3 4·6         2 6·4         3 7·5
   −1 2·8        −1 2·6        −1 7·8
```

```
2   T U t     5   T U t     8   T U t
    3 2·7         4 7·2         8 6·3
   −1 3·9        −2 3·8        −2 9·7
```

```
3   T U t     6   T U t     9   T U t
    4 3·5         4 5·6         5 4·2
   −1 9·7        −2 8·8        −1 6·5
```

D Work out the **difference** between:

```
☆ 12·5 and 1·7    1 2·5
                 −  1·7
                 ──────
                  1 0·8
```

1 14·6 and 2·8   5 6·4 and 14·3

2 11·7 and 3·9   6 18·7 and 23·2

3 26·2 and 15·6   7 26·8 and 14·9

4 21·1 and 9·5   8 20·6 and 32·1

Decimals

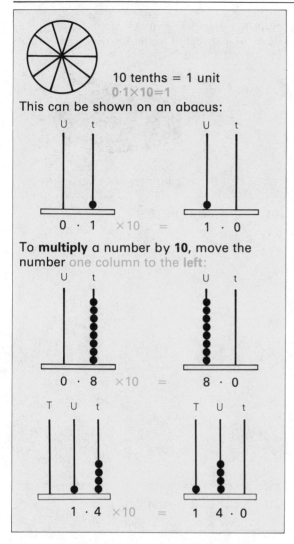

10 tenths = 1 unit
0·1×10=1

This can be shown on an abacus:

0 · 1 ×10 = 1 · 0

To **multiply** a number by **10**, move the number one column to the **left**:

0 · 8 ×10 = 8 · 0

1 · 4 ×10 = 1 4 · 0

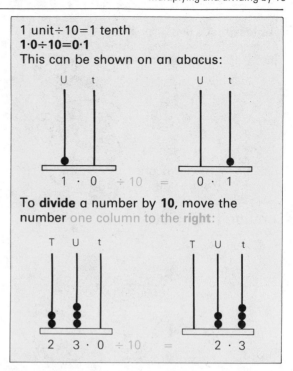

1 unit÷10=1 tenth
1·0÷10=0·1
This can be shown on an abacus:

1 · 0 ÷ 10 = 0 · 1

To **divide** a number by **10**, move the number one column to the **right**:

2 3 · 0 ÷ 10 = 2 · 3

A Multiply the number shown on each abacus by **10**. Draw an abacus to show your answer:

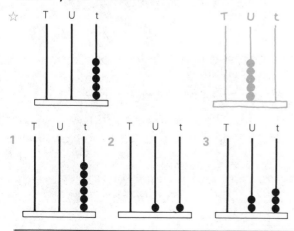

☆

1   2   3

B Divide the number shown on each abacus by **10**. Draw an abacus to show your answer:

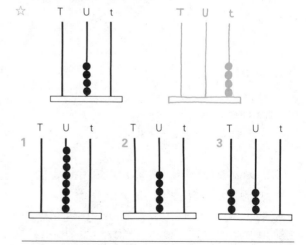

☆

1   2   3

C Write answers only:

☆ 23·0÷10= ✳   2·3

1 0·3×10= ✳   5 1·9×10= ✳

2 2·4×10= ✳   6 14·0÷10= ✳

3 2·0÷10= ✳   7 2·8×10= ✳

4 16·0÷10= ✳   8 86·0÷10= ✳

68 **Decimals**

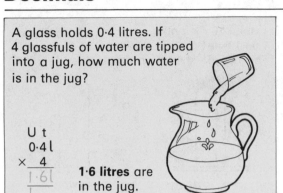

A glass holds 0·4 litres. If 4 glassfuls of water are tipped into a jug, how much water is in the jug?

```
  U t
  0·4 l
×    4
 1·6 l
   1
```

1·6 litres are in the jug.

Ropes are sold in lengths of 12·8 metres. What is the total length of 3 ropes?

```
  T U t
  1 2·8 m
×      3
 3 8·4 m
     2
```

The total length is 38·4 metres.

A Copy and complete:

☆
```
  T U t
  1 3·4
×     5
```
```
  T U t
  1 3·4
×     5
 6 7·0
```

1
```
  U t
  0·3
×   4
```
2
```
  U t
  0·7
×   4
```
3
```
  T U t
  1 2·5
×     3
```
4
```
  T U t
  1 4·6
×     4
```
5
```
  T U t
  2 4·3
×     4
```
6
```
  T U t
  1 7·5
×     6
```

C Copy and complete:

☆
```
  T U t
  1 5·7
×     4
```
```
  T U t
  1 5·7
×     4
 6 2·8
```

1
```
  T U t
  2 1·5
×     3
```
2
```
  T U t
  2 4·3
×     5
```
3
```
  T U t
  2 4·9
×     3
```
4
```
  T U t
  1 2·3
×     8
```
5
```
  T U t
  2 3·7
×     4
```
6
```
  T U t
  1 6·5
×     6
```

B Answer these questions:

☆ 4 tables each 2·3 m long are placed end to end. What is the total length of the tables?
```
  2·3 m
×    4
 9·2 m
```

1 Cakes weigh 1·6 kg. What is the total weight of 5 cakes?

2 A swimming pool is 23·5 metres long. Ben swims 4 lengths. How far does he swim?

3 Petrol cans hold 4·3 litres. How much petrol is there in 10 cans?

D Answer these questions:

☆ A gorilla eats 2·4 kg of bananas each day. What weight of bananas does the gorilla eat in one week?
```
  2·4 kg
×    7
 16·8 kg
```

1 A camel drinks 2·5 litres of water 3 times during the day. How much water does the camel drink?

2 It takes 23·5 minutes to make a toy. How long does it take to make 10 toys?

3 Packs of dog biscuits weigh 2·3 kg each. What is the weight of 10 packs?

Decimals

division, one place of decimals 69

A piece of string measures 9·6 cm.
If it is cut into 3 equal pieces, what
will be the length of each piece?

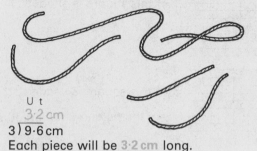

```
    U t
    3·2 cm
3) 9·6 cm
```
Each piece will be **3·2 cm** long.

Simon's garden is 218·6 m long.
Billy's garden is half this length. How
long is Billy's garden?

```
   H T u t
   1 0 9·3 m
2) 2 1 8·6 m
```
Billy's garden is **109·3 m** long.

A house is 9·6 m high.
The door is ¼ of this height.
How high is the door?

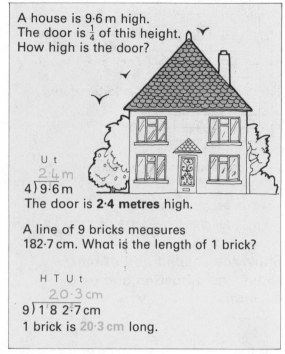

```
    U t
    2·4 m
4) 9·6 m
```
The door is **2·4 metres** high.

A line of 9 bricks measures
182·7 cm. What is the length of 1 brick?

```
   H T U t
   2 0·3 cm
9) 1 8 2·7 cm
```
1 brick is **20·3 cm** long.

A Copy and complete:

```
   H T U t              1 0 7·2
 ☆ 4) 4 2 8·8        4) 4 2 8·8
```

```
     T U t          T U t           T U t
1  5) 8 5·5     4  3) 6 0·9     7  5) 4 7·0
```

```
     T U t          H T U t         T U t
2  4) 3 6·8     5  8) 2 4 0·8   8  9) 6 0·3
```

```
     T U t          H T U t         T U t
3  3) 5 4·6     6  4) 1 2 8·8   9  7) 5 1·1
```

B Use **division** to answer these
questions:

☆ What length is ¼ of 84·8 m?
```
                      2 1·2 m
                   4) 8 4·8 m
```

1 What weight is ⅕ of 65·5 kg?

2 What capacity is ⅓ of 90·6 litres?

3 What length is ½ of 326·8 cm?

4 What weight is ⅙ of 750·6 grams?

5 What capacity is ¼ of 372·4 millilitres?

C Copy and complete:

```
   H T U t                1 2 6·6
 ☆ 5) 6 3 3·0          5) 6 3 3·0
```

```
     U t          T U t            H T U t
1  3) 8·1     3  5) 2 6·0      5  6) 8 1 2·4
```

```
     U t          T U t            H T U t
2  8) 6·4     4  4) 5 7·6      6  7) 3 2 5·5
```

D Answer these questions:

☆ A cake weighs 5·4 kg.
What is the weight of
half of the cake?
```
                2·7 kg
             2) 5·4 kg
```

1 A piece of string is 69·2 metres long.
Fred uses a ¼ of the string. What
length does he use?

2 A paddling pool holds 996·5 litres of
water. How much water is in the pool
when it is ⅕ full?

3 Mr Paddle had 132·8 litres of diesel
fuel in his boat. After 1 day he had
used ⅛ of the fuel. How much fuel
had he used?

This square has been divided into **100** equal parts. Each small square is **one hundredth** of the large square.

You can show this as a fraction: $\frac{1}{100}$ or as a decimal: 0·01

$\frac{7}{100}$ can be written as 0·07

$\frac{23}{100}$ can be written as 0·23

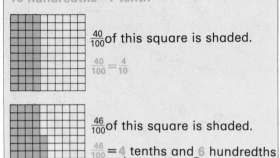

10 hundredths=1 tenth

$\frac{40}{100}$ of this square is shaded.

$\frac{40}{100}=\frac{4}{10}$

$\frac{46}{100}$ of this square is shaded.

$\frac{46}{100}=4$ tenths and 6 hundredths

$\frac{46}{100}=0\cdot46$

A Show the shaded part of these shapes as a **fraction** and as a **decimal**:

    $\frac{45}{100}$ 0·45

 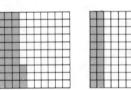

1   3   5

2   4   6

B Write these fractions as **decimals**:

☆ $\frac{16}{100}$ 0·16

1 $\frac{24}{100}$ 4 $\frac{63}{100}$ 7 $\frac{83}{100}$

2 $\frac{37}{100}$ 5 $\frac{94}{100}$ 8 $\frac{21}{100}$

3 $\frac{42}{100}$ 6 $\frac{70}{100}$ 9 $\frac{17}{100}$

C Copy and complete:

☆ $\frac{30}{100}=\frac{*}{10}$ $\frac{30}{100}=\frac{3}{10}$

1 $\frac{50}{100}=\frac{*}{10}$ 5 $\frac{90}{100}=\frac{*}{10}$

2 $\frac{80}{100}=\frac{*}{10}$ 6 $\frac{20}{100}=\frac{*}{10}$

3 $\frac{70}{100}=\frac{*}{10}$ 7 $\frac{60}{100}=\frac{*}{10}$

4 $\frac{10}{100}=\frac{*}{10}$ 8 $\frac{40}{100}=\frac{*}{10}$

D Write these as **tenths** and **hundredths**:

☆ $\frac{52}{100}$ 5 tenths 2 hundredths

1 $\frac{43}{100}$ 4 $\frac{62}{100}$ 7 $\frac{35}{100}$

2 $\frac{16}{100}$ 5 $\frac{97}{100}$ 8 $\frac{59}{100}$

3 $\frac{29}{100}$ 6 $\frac{11}{100}$ 9 $\frac{68}{100}$

E Write as a **decimal**:

☆ 8 tenths 3 hundredths   0·83

1 7 tenths 4 hundredths

2 2 tenths 7 hundredths

3 9 tenths 6 hundredths

4 1 tenth 2 hundredths

5 0 tenths 9 hundredths

6 3 tenths 0 hundredths

7 5 tenths 5 hundredths

8 6 tenths 9 hundredths

9 2 tenths 3 hundredths

10 9 tenths 9 hundredths

Decimals

How many squares are shaded?

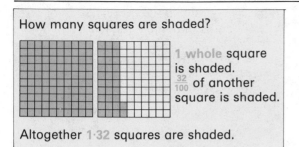

1 whole square is shaded. $\frac{32}{100}$ of another square is shaded.

Altogether **1·32** squares are shaded.

100 hundredths make 1 unit

132 hundredths =
   1 unit and **32** hundredths or **1·32**

223 hundredths =
   2 units and **23** hundredths or **2·23**

A How many squares are shaded in each group below?

☆
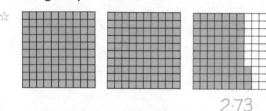
2·73

1
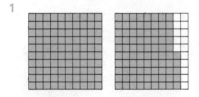

2
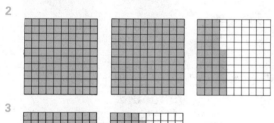

3

4
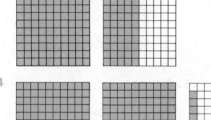

B Write these amounts as **decimals**:

☆ $2\frac{63}{100}$ 2·63

1 $3\frac{56}{100}$ 3 $4\frac{78}{100}$ 5 $5\frac{47}{100}$

2 $2\frac{81}{100}$ 4 $3\frac{69}{100}$ 6 $3\frac{6}{100}$

C How many **hundredths** make:

☆ 2 units?   200

1 3 units?   5 9 units?
2 5 units?   6 10 units?
3 4 units?   7 6 units?
4 7 units?   8 8 units?

D Write these as **decimals**:

☆ 184 hundredths   1·84

1 153 hundredths   6 197 hundredths
2 176 hundredths   7 625 hundredths
3 224 hundredths   8 496 hundredths
4 287 hundredths   9 209 hundredths
5 324 hundredths   10 307 hundredths

E Write these in order, **smallest first**:

☆ 2·74   1·63   0·28   2·47   3·85
   0·28   1·63   2·47   2·74   3·85

1   1·65   1·82   1·79   1·43   1·96
2   3·47   3·43   3·41   3·49   3·45
3   1·76   7·61   7·76   1·67   7·16
4   8·82   2·28   3·82   2·83   8·79
5   2·46   3·46   6·42   6·24   6·46
6   5·93   6·02   5·39   6·21   1·26
7   3·83   3·44   4·33   4·34   4·44
8   6·26   6·62   2·66   2·26   2·22
9   0·72   0·22   0·27   0·77   0·70
10   1·11   1·01   0·11   0·01   0·10

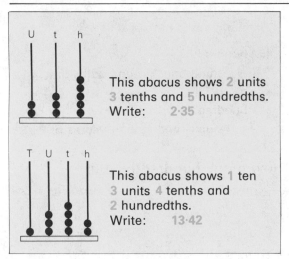

This abacus shows 2 units 3 tenths and 5 hundredths.
Write: 2·35

This abacus shows 1 ten 3 units 4 tenths and 2 hundredths.
Write: 13·42

$\frac{46}{100}$ = 4 tenths and 6 hundredths
or 0·46
This can be shown on an abacus:

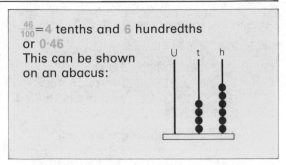

A Write the number shown on each abacus in 2 different ways:

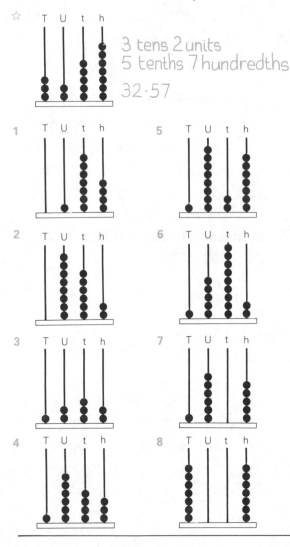

☆ 3 tens 2 units
5 tenths 7 hundredths

32·57

B Draw abacus pictures to show:

☆ 14·07

1 9·54   4 3·07

2 12·65   5 20·62

3 0·23   6 42·09

C Draw abacus pictures to show:

☆ $\frac{58}{100}$

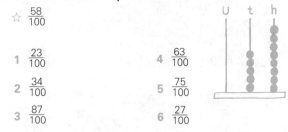

1 $\frac{23}{100}$ 4 $\frac{63}{100}$

2 $\frac{34}{100}$ 5 $\frac{75}{100}$

3 $\frac{87}{100}$ 6 $\frac{27}{100}$

D Write the value of each abacus number in **hundredths**:

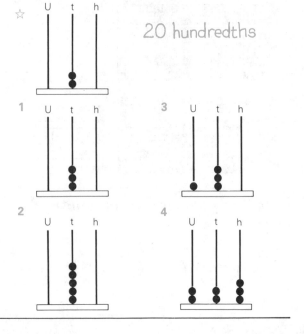

☆ 20 hundredths

A Copy and complete.
Write numbers for ✱'s:

1 $\frac{3}{4}=\frac{✱}{8}$

2 $\frac{1}{3}=\frac{✱}{6}$

3 $\frac{3}{5}=\frac{✱}{10}$

4 $\frac{1}{2}=\frac{3}{✱}$

5 $\frac{4}{5}=\frac{✱}{10}$

6 $\frac{1}{4}=\frac{2}{✱}$

7 $\frac{6}{10}=\frac{✱}{5}$

8 $\frac{2}{6}=\frac{1}{✱}$

B Copy and complete:

1 $\frac{2}{5}+\frac{3}{5}=$ ✱

2 $\frac{4}{10}+\frac{3}{10}=$ ✱

3 $\frac{3}{4}+\frac{1}{8}=$ ✱

4 $\frac{2}{5}+\frac{1}{10}=$ ✱

5 $\frac{1}{6}+\frac{2}{3}=$ ✱

6 $\frac{1}{5}+\frac{3}{10}=$ ✱

7 $\frac{1}{3}+\frac{7}{12}=$ ✱

8 $\frac{5}{6}+\frac{1}{12}=$ ✱

C Work out:

1 $\frac{1}{8}$ of 40

2 $\frac{1}{4}$ of 36

3 $\frac{1}{6}$ of 54

4 $\frac{1}{7}$ of 49

5 $\frac{1}{5}$ of 45

6 $\frac{1}{12}$ of 48

7 $\frac{3}{10}$ of 100

8 $\frac{2}{9}$ of 81

9 $\frac{5}{8}$ of 56

10 $\frac{3}{4}$ of 48

D

1 Jane had £48. She spent $\frac{3}{8}$ of this on some records. How much did the records cost?

2 There are 54 litres of petrol in a car. If $\frac{5}{6}$ of the petrol is used for a journey, how much petrol is left?

3 A bakery sold 185 cakes. If $\frac{4}{5}$ of the cakes were doughnuts, how many doughnuts were sold?

4 96 cars were made at a factory. If $\frac{2}{3}$ of the cars were estate cars, how many were **not** estate cars?

E Write these fractions as **decimals**:

1 $\frac{8}{10}$

2 $\frac{6}{10}$

3 $\frac{9}{10}$

4 $\frac{5}{10}$

5 $\frac{16}{100}$

6 $\frac{19}{100}$

7 $\frac{26}{100}$

8 $\frac{32}{100}$

9 $\frac{7}{10}$

10 $\frac{72}{100}$

11 $\frac{86}{100}$

12 $\frac{41}{100}$

F Write these decimals as **fractions**:

1 0·4

2 0·8

3 0·7

4 0·1

5 1·7

6 2·8

7 3·6

8 8·4

9 0·36

10 0·28

11 0·71

12 0·89

G Copy and complete:

1
```
  T U t
  6 2·3
+ 1 7·9
```

2
```
  T U t
  5 2·7
+ 2 6·9
```

3
```
  T U t
  4 7·3
− 1 6·7
```

4
```
  T U t
  5 4·6
+ 2 5·7
```

5
```
  T U t
  3 8·6
− 1 9·9
```

6
```
  T U t
  3 6·4
− 1 9·7
```

H Copy and complete:

1
```
  T U t
  1 5·6
×     4
```

2
```
  T U t
  1 8·5
×     7
```

3
```
  T U t
  2 2·6
×     4
```

4
```
  T U t
6)8 2·2
```

5
```
  T U t
5)6 7·0
```

6
```
  T u t
8)9 2·8
```

I Write numbers for ✱'s:

1 $0·6×10=$ ✱

2 $0·9×10=$ ✱

3 $1·3×10=$ ✱

4 $2·7×10=$ ✱

5 $15·0÷10=$ ✱

6 $36·0÷10=$ ✱

7 $28·0÷10=$ ✱

8 $57·0÷10=$ ✱

J Write these in order, **smallest first**:

1 0·5 3·6 0·1 6·3 3·3

2 7·2 2·1 7·8 1·2 2·7

3 5·6 5·2 5·9 5·1 5·7

4 6·83 6·38 8·63 8·36 6·36

5 19·56 19·65 15·69 16·95 19·55

A You need five pieces of thick paper or thin card all measuring 3 cm by 4 cm. You also need a partner.

Write down the five different numbers you could show on this abacus using 4 beads each time.

Write each number on one of your pieces of card.

Shuffle the cards and lay them down in a line.

 ←

By moving one card at a time to the beginning or end of the line, arrange the cards in order of size with the smallest number on the left and the largest number on the right. Count how many cards you need to move to do this.

Your partner now has a turn and tries to place the cards in order taking less moves than you.

The player who takes fewer moves scores a point. If both players take the same number of moves then both players score a point.

Continue to take turns until one player has scored 5 points.

This player is the winner.

Repeat the activity with this abacus using
a) 2 beads   b) 3 beads

Example **3·1**

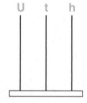

B To show $\frac{1}{10}$ as a decimal you write 0·1. You can check this by entering **1 ÷ 10 =** into your calculator.

Use your calculator to change these fractions to decimals:

$\frac{1}{2}$ $\frac{1}{4}$ $\frac{1}{8}$ $\frac{1}{5}$ $\frac{3}{5}$ $\frac{7}{10}$ $\frac{4}{5}$ $\frac{3}{4}$ $\frac{3}{10}$ $\frac{3}{8}$ $\frac{2}{5}$ $\frac{5}{8}$ $\frac{7}{8}$ $\frac{1}{100}$ $\frac{17}{100}$ $\frac{43}{100}$ $\frac{50}{100}$ $\frac{20}{100}$ $\frac{35}{100}$

What happens when you change these fractions to decimals?

$\frac{1}{3}$ $\frac{1}{6}$ $\frac{1}{7}$ $\frac{1}{9}$ $\frac{5}{6}$ $\frac{3}{7}$ $\frac{8}{9}$ $\frac{2}{3}$

Work out which is the smaller fraction in each pair below by changing both fractions to decimals.

a) $\frac{5}{8}$ $\frac{4}{5}$ b) $\frac{3}{4}$ $\frac{7}{10}$ c) $\frac{5}{7}$ $\frac{7}{9}$ d) $\frac{2}{3}$ $\frac{5}{8}$ e) $\frac{3}{5}$ $\frac{4}{7}$ f) $\frac{59}{100}$ $\frac{5}{9}$

Write down two different fractions that you think are about the same size. Use your calculator to check which fraction is the smaller.

Repeat this for five more pairs of fractions.

Answer any questions you can. Leave those you cannot do.

Show as a decimal the coloured part of each shape:

1

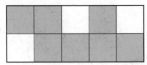

2

3

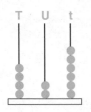

Write these decimals as fractions:

4 0·9

5 0·73

Write these fractions as decimals:

6 $\frac{3}{10}$

7 $\frac{32}{100}$

Write as a decimal the number shown on each abacus:

8

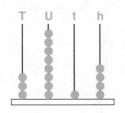

9

Copy and complete:

10	1 6·4	11	2 9·7
	+ 2 3·5		+ 3 8·5

12 Three tanks hold 84·3 l, 39·7 l and 41·5 l. How much water can the three tanks hold all together?

Copy and complete:

13   1 5·7
    − 1 0·4

14   1 8 3·8
     −   3 9·9

15   5 6 2·1
     − 3 9 0·7

16 What is the difference in weight between two cases weighing 58·7 kg and 81·4 kg?

Copy and complete:

17   3·9   18   2 3·7
    ×   9   ×   9

19 What is the total capacity of 6 barrels each of which hold 64·6 litres?

Copy and complete:

20 $5\overline{)63·5}$ 21 $8\overline{)123·2}$

22 A car's tank can hold 42·8 litres of petrol. If $\frac{1}{4}$ of the fuel is used, how much is left?

Write numbers for ✳'s:

23 2·9 × 10 = ✳

24 14·7 × 10 = ✳

25 6·85 × 10 = ✳

26 9·0 ÷ 10 = ✳

27 6·3 ÷ 10 = ✳

100 pence = £1
1p = one hundredth of £1
Write: **1p = £0·01**

26p = £0·26
82p = £0·82

A Write these amounts as **pounds**:

☆ £0·87

1

2

3

4

B Write these amounts as **pounds**:

☆ £1·75

1

2

3

C Write coins to pay for each item:

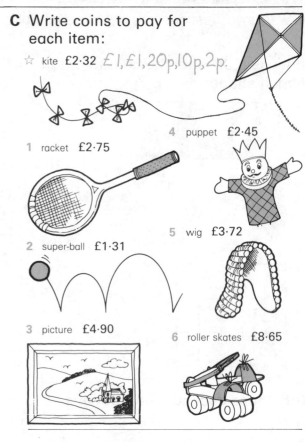

☆ kite £2·32 £1, £1, 20p, 10p, 2p.

1 racket £2·75

2 super-ball £1·31

3 picture £4·90

4 puppet £2·45

5 wig £3·72

6 roller skates £8·65

D Copy and complete.
Show coins to pay each amount:

		£1	50p	20p	10p	5p	2p	1p
☆	£2·36	2		l	l	l		l
1	£3·92							
2	£1·63							
3	£3·85							
4	£5·22							

E Copy and complete:

	cost	money given	change
☆	13p	20p	7p
1	29p	50p	
2	64p	£1	
3	85p	£1	
4	£1·93	£5	

Money

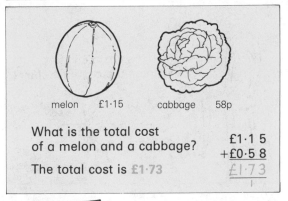

melon £1·15   cabbage 58p

What is the total cost
of a melon and a cabbage?

The total cost is **£1·73**

$$\begin{array}{r} £1·15 \\ +£0·58 \\ \hline £1·73 \end{array}$$

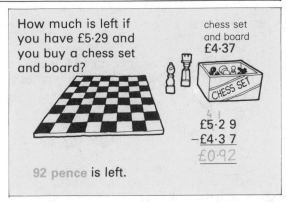

How much is left if
you have £5·29 and
you buy a chess set
and board?

chess set
and board
£4·37

$$\begin{array}{r} £5·29 \\ -£4·37 \\ \hline £0·92 \end{array}$$

92 pence is left.

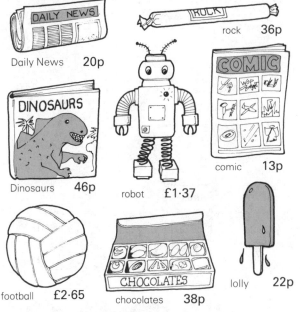

rock 36p

Daily News 20p

comic 13p

Dinosaurs 46p

robot £1·37

lolly 22p

football £2·65

chocolates 38p

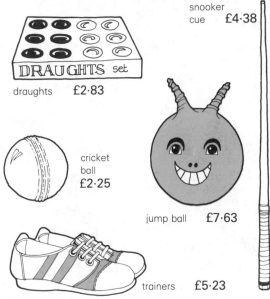

snooker
cue £4·38

draughts £2·83

cricket
ball
£2·25

jump ball £7·63

trainers £5·23

A Work out the cost of:

☆ a football and a book   £3·11

1 a newspaper and some chocolates

2 a stick of rock and a robot

3 a football and some chocolates

4 a robot, a comic and a lolly

5 a football, a robot and a comic

B What change will you get if you give:

☆ 20p for a comic?   7p

1 £1 for a dinosaur book?

2 £3 for a football?

3 50p for a lolly?

4 £1 for a stick of rock?

C How much is left if:

☆ you have £3·91 and
you buy a draughts game?

£1·08

1 you have £5·27 and you buy a snooker
cue?

2 you have £9·57 and you buy a jump
ball?

3 you have £7·20 and you buy a pair of
training shoes?

4 you have £5·80 and you buy a cricket
ball?

5 you have £3·00 and you buy a
draughts game?

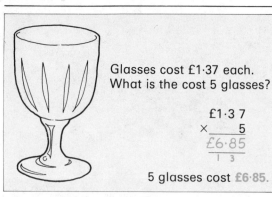

Glasses cost £1·37 each.
What is the cost 5 glasses?

$$\begin{array}{r} £1·37 \\ \times \quad 5 \\ \hline £6·85 \\ \scriptstyle 1\ 3 \end{array}$$

5 glasses cost **£6·85**.

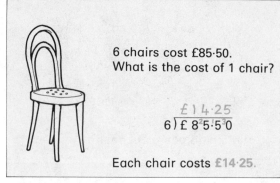

6 chairs cost £85·50.
What is the cost of 1 chair?

$$\begin{array}{r} £14·25 \\ 6\overline{)£8\,{}^{2}5·{}^{5}0} \end{array}$$

Each chair costs **£14·25**.

A Work out the cost of:

☆ 4 beachballs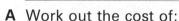

£1·35 each

$$\begin{array}{r} £1·35 \\ \times \quad 4 \\ \hline £5·40 \end{array}$$

1 8 meals of fish and chips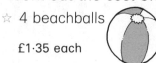

£1·33 each

2 3 pens

£1·65 each

3 4 torches

£2·86 each

4 5 pairs of scissors

£2·29 each

5 10 books

£1·32 each

6 7 mats

£2·37 each

B Copy and complete:

☆
$$\begin{array}{r} £2·63 \\ \times \quad 5 \\ \hline \end{array}$$
$$\begin{array}{r} £2·63 \\ \times \quad 5 \\ \hline £13·15 \end{array}$$

1
$$\begin{array}{r} £4·53 \\ \times \quad 6 \\ \hline \end{array}$$

2
$$\begin{array}{r} £2·73 \\ \times \quad 5 \\ \hline \end{array}$$

3
$$\begin{array}{r} £3·55 \\ \times \quad 7 \\ \hline \end{array}$$

4
$$\begin{array}{r} £4·26 \\ \times \quad 6 \\ \hline \end{array}$$

5
$$\begin{array}{r} £2·99 \\ \times \quad 2 \\ \hline \end{array}$$

6
$$\begin{array}{r} £5·49 \\ \times \quad 5 \\ \hline \end{array}$$

C Work out the cost of:

☆ 1 CD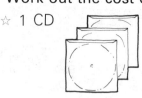

set of 3   £9·87

$$\begin{array}{r} £3·29 \\ 3\overline{)£9·87} \end{array}$$

1 1 plate

set of 9   £12·87

2 1 battery

set of 4 £1·84

3 1 tyre

set of 4   £74·60

4 1 stool

set of 3   £36·78

D Copy and complete:

☆ $4\overline{)£46·24}$ $\begin{array}{r} £11·56 \\ 4\overline{)£46·24} \end{array}$

1 $3\overline{)£37·02}$

2 $6\overline{)£75·18}$

3 $7\overline{)£39·76}$

4 $9\overline{)£92·25}$

5 $5\overline{)£68·45}$

6 $8\overline{)£53·44}$

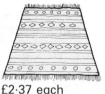

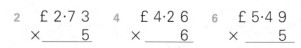

Money

On holiday
The Lucky family are going on
holiday to Brighton.

MENU

Soup 45p	
Melon 52p	Cheese and Egg
Fruit Juice 38p	Salad £1.28
	Ice-cream 38p
Roast Beef and	Trifle 53p
Vegetables £1.85	Tea 17p
Ravioli £1.08	Coffee 24p
	Coke 25p

A Work out the cost of:

☆ 2 adult train fares

```
  £5·26
x     2
 £10·52
```

TICKETS

BRIGHTON
adults £5·26
children £2·66

1 3 child's train fares

2 A ham roll and tea
for Mr Lucky

3 A ham roll and coffee
for Mrs Lucky

SEA FRONT
CAFE
MENU

Ham Roll	38p
Pastie	36p
Crisps	12p
Tea	18p
Coffee	24p
Coke	25p

4 A pastie and a coke
for Matthew

5 2 packets of crisps
and a coke for Lucy

6 A pastie and tea for Polly

7 3 buckets and
2 spades

spades 87p   buckets 65p

8 A boat trip for Mrs
Lucky, Polly and Matthew 𝛾

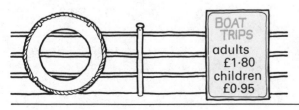

BOAT TRIPS
adults £1·80
children £0·95

B Work out these bills:

☆
```
2 soups          £0·90
3 roast beef     £5·55
2 ice cream      £0·76
                 £7·21
```

1
1 soup
1 ravioli
1 trifle
1 coffee

4
1 fruit juice
1 salad
1 ice cream
2 teas

2
1 melon
1 fruit juice
1 ravioli
1 salad
1 trifle
1 tea

5
2 melon
1 fruit juice
3 salads
3 ice cream
3 cakes

3
2 soups
2 roast beef
2 trifles
2 coffees

6
3 soups
3 ravioli
3 ice cream
1 trifle
3 coffees

This is your money:

This is your money:

A Can you give the exact money?
Say **yes** or **no**:

☆ £1.27

scissors

yes

1 £2·93   ring

2 £1·26   key

3 £1·58   candle

4 73p   ball

5 £1·84   purse

6 89p   pickles

BEST PICKLES

B Use your money shown above.
Copy and complete this table:

	cost	coins you would give	change
☆	£1·99	£1 £1	1p
1	£1·64		
2	£1·46		
3	£2·59		
4	£3·29		
5	£1·92		
6	£2·89		

C Can you afford:

☆ 3 puppets at £1·90 each?

$$\begin{array}{r} £1·90 \\ \times\quad 3 \\ \hline £5·70 \end{array}$$

no

1 2 footballs at £2·20 each?

2 3 T-shirts at £1·60 each?

3 A pen costing £2·45 and a hat costing £2·08?

4 3 records costing £1·50 each?

5 5 biros each costing 82p?

6 2 books at £2·19 each?

7 A scarf costing £1·99, a record token for £1·10 and 3 pencils costing 15p each?

8 Three pictures each costing 75p, and three frames each costing 79p?

D Answer these questions:

☆ Jess buys 5 ice creams costing 18p each. How much change does she receive from £1?   *10p*

1 John buys some string and receives 42p change from £1. What was the cost of the string?

2 Mrs Green buys 5 concert tickets costing £2·34 each. How much does she spend?

3 Mr Read buys 3 books each costing £1·27. How much change does he receive from £5?

4 It costs £6·75 for 9 children to go to the zoo. What is the cost for each child?

A This machine has been designed so that it will only deliver chocolates when four coins are put in.

Write down the different amounts from 10p to £4 that will operate this machine.

Another machine will only work if silver coins are put in.

Write down the different amounts from 10p to £2 that will operate this machine.

Design a machine for selling meals. Draw a picture of your design.

Write down 8 meals costing less than £5 including the 4 on this list, and write the prices for the meals.

If your machine will accept only £5 notes, work out the amount of change it will need to give with each meal.

Work out the fewest number of coins it can give for each set of change.

Lasagne	£2.58
Roast chicken	£4.75
Fish and chips	£3.25
Beans on toast	£1.64

B

Mrs. Peters is selling raffle tickets. She has tickets numbered from 1 to 100 in a bag and she will give a money prize to anyone who picks out a ticket ending with a '0'.

The prize for ticket number 100 can be different from the prize for other tickets ending in 0. If she charges 20p for each ticket, work out the value of the prizes she can give so that she raises more than £10 but less than £15 for the school funds.

Mr. Ahmed is selling another set of tickets numbered from 1 to 200. He wants to give one prize of £5 and other prizes of £1 and 50p. If he charges 20p for tickets, work out how he can award the prizes so that he raises more than £20 but less than £25 for the school funds.

Devise a game for a school fair which would raise money for school funds. You will need to make your game and test it and work out how much to charge for each turn.

Design a game for a school fair so that for every pound taken it would raise 20p for school funds?

Answer any questions you can. Leave those you cannot do.

Write these amounts as pounds:

1

2

Write coins to pay for each item below:

3

Plane £4.63

4

Video £4.65

£7.58　　£6.85　　£5.42　　£6.22

Work out the cost of:

5 a pair of binoculars and a CD

6 a cassette and a hat

7 a hat and a CD

How much change do you receive from £10 when you buy:

8 a CD?

9 a pair of binoculars?

10 a hat?

11 How much is left if you have £8.64 and you buy a hat?

12 How much is left is you have £10.32 and you buy a pair of binoculars?

13 How much is left if you have £8.03 and you buy a cassette?

£1.22　　£0.78　　£1.18　　£1.26

What is the cost of:

14 3 colas?

15 5 burgers?

16 4 ice creams?

17 2 portions of chips and 2 colas?

18 A man pays £5.46 for bottles of cola. How many bottles does he buy?

19 Jimmy pays £6.06 for 2 portions of ice cream and some chips. How many portions of chips does he buy?

Work out the total cost of:

20 1 CD if 3 CD's cost £17.64

21 1 stool if 4 stools cost £93.28

Copy and complete:

22
```
  £ 2.5 6
+ £ 4.8 5
```

23
```
  £ 5.2 7
− £ 2.3 8
```

24
```
  £ 4.2 9
×       6
```

25 7) £47.81

Length

A Copy this table:

line	estimate (cm)	measure (cm)	difference (cm)
1			
2			
3			
4			
5			
6			

line 1   line 2   line 3   line 4   line 5   line 6

C You need a length of string.
Work out the length of each snail trail, to the nearest centimetre:

Crawley 23cm

B 1 Estimate in centimetres the length of line 1.

2 Write the estimate in your table.

3 Measure line 1.

4 Write the measure in your table.

5 Work out the difference between your estimate and the measure.

6 Write the difference in the table.

7 Do the same for each of the other lines.

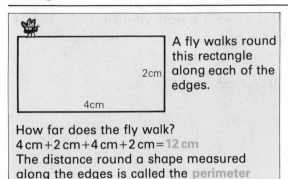

A fly walks round this rectangle along each of the edges.

How far does the fly walk?
4 cm + 2 cm + 4 cm + 2 cm = 12 cm
The distance round a shape measured along the edges is called the perimeter of the shape.

B Copy this table:

shape	perimeter (cm)		
	estimate (cm)	measure (cm)	difference (cm)
triangle			
parallel-ogram			
square			
rectangle			
pentagon			

A How far would a fly walk if it walked round the **perimeter** of each of these shapes?

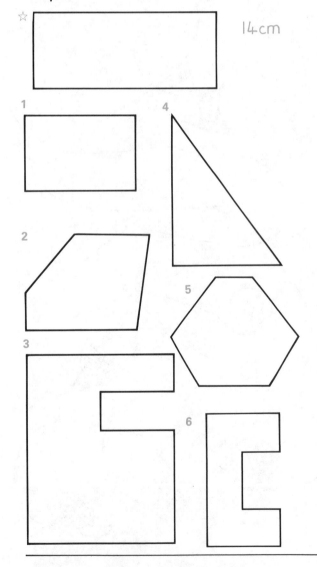

14 cm

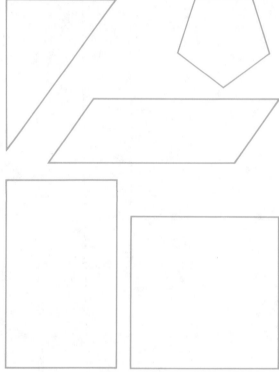

C 1 Estimate in centimetres the perimeter of the triangle.

2 Write the estimate in your table.

3 Measure the perimeter.

4 Write the measure in your table.

5 Work out the difference between your estimate and the measure.

6 Write the difference in the table.

7 Do the same for each of the other shapes.

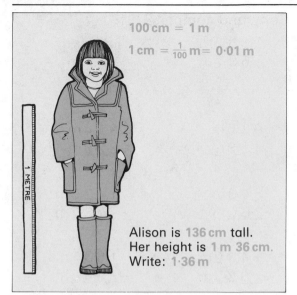

100 cm = 1 m

1 cm = $\frac{1}{100}$ m = 0.01 m

Alison is 136 cm tall.
Her height is 1 m 36 cm.
Write: 1.36 m

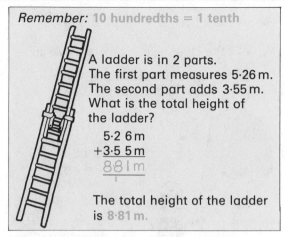

Remember: 10 hundredths = 1 tenth

A ladder is in 2 parts.
The first part measures 5·26 m.
The second part adds 3·55 m.
What is the total height of
the ladder?

```
  5·2 6 m
+ 3·5 5 m
  8.8 1 m
```

The total height of the ladder
is 8.81 m.

A Write these heights in **metres**:

☆ 1 m 84 cm   1·84 m

1 1 m 62 cm   6 2 m 45 cm
2 185 cm   7 3 m 22 cm
3 1 m 74 cm   8 249 cm
4 139 cm   9 283 cm
5 186 cm   10 325 cm

B Write these lengths in **metres** and **centimetres**:

☆ 3·64 m   3 metres 64 centimetres

1 2·52 m   6 3·06 m
2 1·87 m   7 4·09 m
3 4·56 m   8 12·63 m
4 9·83 m   9 19·02 m
5 2·70 m   10 15·66 m

C Write these lengths in **centimetres**:

☆ 2·59 m   259 cm

1 1·12 m   6 4·68 m
2 3·85 m   7 1·57 m
3 2·36 m   8 3·46 m
4 4·24 m   9 2·51 m
5 5·92 m   10 6·49 m

D Work out the total **height** of these ladders:

☆ 1st part 4·27 m
   2nd part adds 2·84 m

```
  4·27 m
+ 2·84 m
  7·11 m
```

1 1st part 3·92 m   4 1st part 3·85 m
   2nd part adds   2nd part adds
   1·86 m   2·63 m

2 1st part 4·53 m   5 1st part 2·94 m
   2nd part adds   2nd part adds
   3·27 m   1·43 m

3 1st part 5·26 m   6 1st part 3·62 m
   2nd part adds   2nd part adds
   3·75 m   2·98 m

E Copy and complete:

```
☆    2·6 5 m          2·65 m
   + 1·9 2 m        + 1·92 m
   ─────────          4·57 m
```

```
1    2·7 4 m    4    3·2 9 m    7    6·4 7 m
   + 3·8 1 m      + 1·7 3 m      + 2·9 3 m
```

```
2    3·2 7 m    5    4·6 3 m    8    5·5 6 m
   + 2·9 2 m      + 4·2 8 m      + 3·9 1 m
```

```
3    4·8 5 m    6    3·8 6 m    9    0·3 9 m
   + 2·8 2 m      + 4·9 9 m      + 7·9 3 m
```

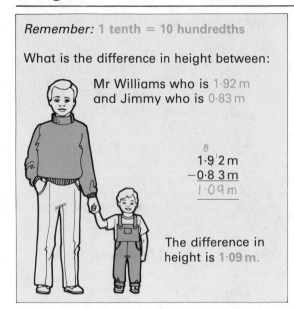

Remember: 1 tenth = 10 hundredths

What is the difference in height between:

Mr Williams who is 1·92 m
and Jimmy who is 0·83 m

$$\begin{array}{r} {}^{8}\ 1·9\overset{1}{2}\,m \\ -\ 0·8\ 3\,m \\ \hline 1·09\,m \end{array}$$

The difference in
height is 1·09 m.

A Work out the **difference in height**
between:

☆ the boat   and the bridge
   height 3·27 m   height 4·63 m

$$\begin{array}{r} 4·63\,m \\ -\ 3·27\,m \\ \hline 1·36\,m \end{array}$$

1 the bus   and the car
  height 5·84 m   height 1·57 m

2 the lamp post   and the fence
  height 8·37 m   height 0·75 m

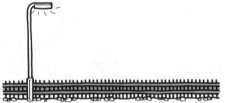

3 the garage   and the house
  height 2·63 m   height 7·59 m

B Copy and complete:

☆
$$\begin{array}{r} 1\ 3·8\ 2\,m \\ -\ 6·9\ 7\,m \\ \hline \end{array}$$
$$\begin{array}{r} 13·82\,m \\ -\ 6·97\,m \\ \hline 6·85\,m \end{array}$$

1
$$\begin{array}{r} 9·3\ 5\,m \\ -4·2\ 8\,m \\ \hline \end{array}$$
7
$$\begin{array}{r} 9·1\ 4\,m \\ -3·2\ 8\,m \\ \hline \end{array}$$

2
$$\begin{array}{r} 8·4\ 3\,m \\ -2·6\ 0\,m \\ \hline \end{array}$$
8
$$\begin{array}{r} 1\ 4·2\ 3\,m \\ -\ 7·3\ 2\,m \\ \hline \end{array}$$

3
$$\begin{array}{r} 1\ 4·3\ 9\,m \\ -\ 6·2\ 7\,m \\ \hline \end{array}$$
9
$$\begin{array}{r} 1\ 6·3\ 1\,m \\ -\ 9·0\ 5\,m \\ \hline \end{array}$$

4
$$\begin{array}{r} 2\ 9·3\ 4\,m \\ -1\ 1·7\ 2\,m \\ \hline \end{array}$$
10
$$\begin{array}{r} 3\ 5·9\ 4\,m \\ -1\ 7·8\ 6\,m \\ \hline \end{array}$$

5
$$\begin{array}{r} 1\ 6·8\ 4\,m \\ -\ 3·9\ 2\,m \\ \hline \end{array}$$
11
$$\begin{array}{r} 1\ 3·4\ 1\,m \\ -\ 8·1\ 9\,m \\ \hline \end{array}$$

6
$$\begin{array}{r} 1\ 4·2\ 4\,m \\ -\ 5·1\ 6\,m \\ \hline \end{array}$$
12
$$\begin{array}{r} 2\ 5·4\ 4\,m \\ -1\ 1·5\ 5\,m \\ \hline \end{array}$$

C Answer these:

	length of roll	length cut off	length left
☆	29·62 m	5·17 m	24·45 m
1	42·35 m	4·06 m	
2	36·92 m	3·49 m	
3	28·66 m	10·72 m	
4	13·95 m	4·78 m	
5	25·67 m	3·99 m	
6	31·79 m	12·87 m	
7	27·63 m	9·72 m	
8	48·07 m	39·25 m	

Length

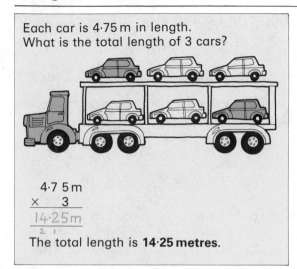

Each car is 4·75 m in length.
What is the total length of 3 cars?

```
  4·7 5 m
×      3
 14·25 m
   2 1
```

The total length is **14·25 metres.**

A Answer these questions:

☆ 1 car is 4·23 metres long. What is the
total length of 6 cars?

```
 4·23 m
×    6
25·38 m
```

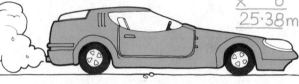

1 1 table is 1·27 metres long. What is
the total length of 4 tables?

2 A container is 3·76 metres high. What
is the total height of 5 containers?

3 A bridge section is 38·52 metres long.
What is the total length of 3 sections?

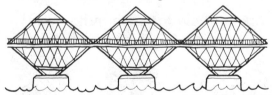

4 Each storey in a block of flats is 3·45
metres high. What is the total height
of 10 storeys?

5 Boxes are 1·03 metres high.
What is the total height of a stack of
7 boxes?

6 8 lengths of rope are needed to
measure the length of a football field.
If each length of rope measures 9·16
metres, how long is the football field?

B Copy and complete:

```
☆   8·7 3 m          8·73 m
   ×     6          ×     6
   _____           52·38 m
```

```
1   7·2 8 m      5   2·9 5 m
   ×     3          ×     2
```

```
2   8·6 2 m      6   1 2·2 7 m
   ×     4          ×      3
```

```
3   4·3 6 m      7   2 4·3 6 m
   ×     4          ×      4
```

```
4   5·7 3 m      8   1 5·6 4 m
   ×     5          ×      6
```

C 1·27 metres of material are needed to
make one netball skirt.
Copy and complete this table:

	number of skirts	metres of material
☆	2	2·54 m
1	3	
2	4	
3	5	
4	8	
5	10	

D A car can travel 12·35 km
using 1 l of petrol.
Copy and complete this table:

	number of litres of petrol	distance car can travel
☆	2	24·7 km
1	3	
2	4	
3	6	
4	8	
5	10	

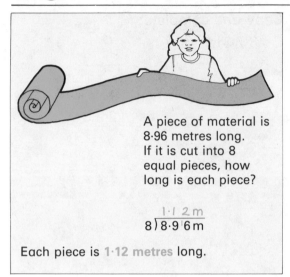

A piece of material is 8·96 metres long. If it is cut into 8 equal pieces, how long is each piece?

$$1·12\,m$$
$$8\overline{)8·9\,6}\,m$$

Each piece is **1·12 metres** long.

A Answer these questions:

☆ A path is made with 9 paving stones. The path is 7·47 metres long. How long is each paving stone?

$$0·83\,m$$
$$9\overline{)7·47}\,m$$

1 A piece of ribbon is 22·76 m long. If it is cut into 4 equal pieces, how long is each piece?

2 4 gardeners are given an equal length of a piece of land. If the land is 93·88 m long, what length of land does each gardener receive?

3 Jason has a length of string measuring 31·92 metres. If he cuts it into 7 equal pieces, how long is each piece?

4 Mr Jones used $\frac{1}{5}$ of a roll of wallpaper. If the roll is 10·25 metres long, how much paper has he used?

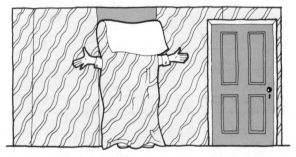

B Copy and complete:

☆ $6\overline{)3·8\,4}\,m$ $\quad$ $0·64\,m$ $6\overline{)3·84}\,m$

1 $2\overline{)5\,9·6\,8}\,m$ $\qquad$ 7 $6\overline{)3\,8·5\,2}\,m$

2 $3\overline{)3\,2·7\,3}\,m$ $\qquad$ 8 $8\overline{)9\,4·6\,4}\,m$

3 $4\overline{)6\,3·5\,6}\,m$ $\qquad$ 9 $9\overline{)6\,5·7\,9}\,m$

4 $3\overline{)4\,2·8\,4}\,m$ $\qquad$ 10 $7\overline{)3\,0·5\,2}\,m$

5 $5\overline{)6\,8·3\,0}\,m$ $\qquad$ 11 $6\overline{)2\,6·3\,4}\,m$

6 $4\overline{)2\,7·4\,4}\,m$ $\qquad$ 12 $10\overline{)9\,1·2\,0}\,m$

C Copy and complete:

	perimeter of square	length of each side
☆	42·88 m	10·72 m
1	48·64 m	
2	32·36 m	
3	27·92 m	
4	52·76 m	
5	11·44 m	
6	85·16 m	
7	92·04 m	
8	61·48 m	

D Work out how far each motorcycle can travel on 1 litre of petrol:

	petrol used	distance travelled	distance per litre
☆	4 l	123·36 km	30·84 km
1	5 l	140·25 km	
2	7 l	225·68 km	
3	10 l	296·80 km	

Length

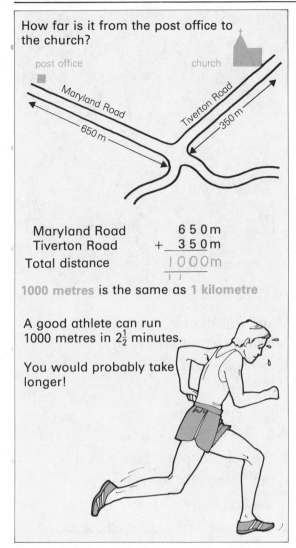

How far is it from the post office to the church?

post office   church

Maryland Road

Tiverton Road

650 m   350 m

Maryland Road	6 5 0 m
Tiverton Road	+ 3 5 0 m
Total distance	1 0 0 0 m

1000 metres is the same as **1 kilometre**

A good athlete can run 1000 metres in $2\frac{1}{2}$ minutes.

You would probably take longer!

This table shows distances from London:

town	distance from London
Chelmsford	52 km
Ilford	18 km
Colchester	89 km
Oxford	90 km
Winchester	103 km

C Copy and complete this graph:

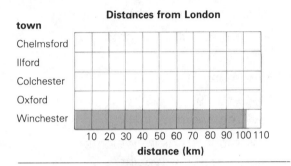

Distances from London

town

Chelmsford
Ilford
Colchester
Oxford
Winchester

10 20 30 40 50 60 70 80 90 100 110
distance (km)

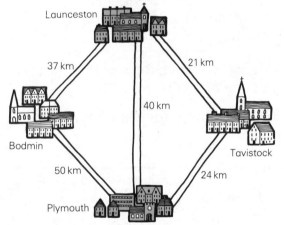

Launceston

37 km   21 km

40 km

Bodmin   Tavistock

50 km   24 km

Plymouth

A Write these distances in **kilometres** and **metres**:

☆ 1384 m   1 km 384 m

1 1246 m   5 2638 m
2 1852 m   6 3726 m
3 1726 m   7 4815 m
4 1405 m   8 5207 m

B Write the sign < or > for ✳'s:

☆ 1268 m ✳ 1 km   >

1 999 m ✳ 1 km   4 2 km ✳ 2500 m
2 1 km ✳ 1045 m   5 3 km ✳ 3050 m
3 1 km ✳ 1111 m   6 5500 m ✳ 5 km

D Work out the **distances** of these journeys:

☆ Bodmin to Tavistock   74 km
   via Plymouth
1 Plymouth to Launceston via Tavistock
2 Launceston to Bodmin via Plymouth
3 Bodmin to Launceston and return
4 Plymouth to Tavistock via Bodmin and Launceston
5 The shortest journey to visit all 4 towns starting from Plymouth

> 1000 grams = 1 kilogram
> 500 grams = $\frac{1}{2}$ kilogram

A Use weights and scales if you need to.

☆ How many 100 g weights balance 1 kilogram?   10

1 How many 10 g weights balance a 50 g weight?

2 How many 100 g weights balance $\frac{1}{2}$ kg?

3 How many 50 g weights balance $\frac{1}{2}$ kg?

4 How many grams in $\frac{1}{2}$ kg?

5 How many 10 gram weights balance a 100 g weight?

6 How many 20 gram weights balance $\frac{1}{2}$ kg?

B This table shows the weights that balance each object.

Work out the total weight for each object:

370 g

	object	1 kg	500 g	100 g	50 g	20 g	10 g
☆	book			3	1	1	
1	tin				1	1	1
2	mug			3	1	2	
3	scissors			1			1
4	vase		1			1	1
5	rubber					1	1
6	cake	1			1	2	
7	marrow	1	1	2			
8	parcel	3	1	1		1	
9	rock	5		2	1	1	
10	case	7		4	1	1	1

gold crown   gold vase   gold watch

956 g   588 g   219 g

gold box   gold coins   gold chain   542 g

486 g   656 g

C Work out the total weight in **kilograms** and **grams** of:

☆ the coins and the vase

$$\begin{array}{r} 656\,g \\ +\ 588\,g \\ \hline 1244\,g \\ \hline \end{array}$$

1 kg 244 g

1 the box and the crown

2 the chain and the box

3 the coins and the box

4 the vase and the chain

5 the box, the coins and the chain

6 the vase, the watch and the crown

7 the box, the vase and the chain

8 the watch, the coins and the crown

D Work out the **difference** in weight between:

☆ the box and the watch

$$\begin{array}{r} 486\,g \\ -\ 219\,g \\ \hline 267\,g \\ \hline \end{array}$$

1 the vase and the chain

2 the coins and the box

3 the crown and the vase

4 the coins and the watch

5 the box and the vase

6 the watch and the crown

Capacity

1000 millilitres = 1 litre

1 litre of lemonade fills ten 100 ml glasses.

100 ml = $\frac{1}{10}$ of a litre
100 ml = 0·1 l

A Write these capacities in **litres** and **millilitres**:

☆ 2635 ml   2 l 635ml

1. 1475 ml
2. 1860 ml
3. 2500 ml
4. 2100 ml
5. 3225 ml
6. 3750 ml
7. 5625 ml
8. 4965 ml

B Write these capacities in **millilitres**:

☆ 0·5 l   500 ml

1. $\frac{1}{10}$ l
2. $\frac{3}{10}$ l
3. 0·7 l
4. $1\frac{1}{2}$ l
5. $\frac{8}{10}$ l
6. 2·1 l
7. $\frac{6}{10}$ l
8. 1·3 l

C How many glassfuls would fill each jug?

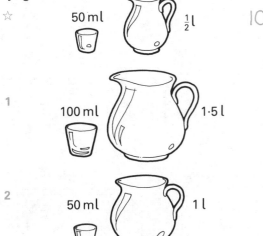

☆   50 ml $\frac{1}{2}$ l   10

1.   100 ml   1·5 l

2.   50 ml   1 l

D How much water would you need to fill all 3 containers?

☆   250 ml $\frac{1}{2}$ litre   100 ml

250 ml
500 ml
+ 100 ml
850 ml

1. $\frac{1}{2}$ litre   250 ml   200 ml

2.   900 ml   1650 ml   2 litres

3.   6$\frac{1}{2}$ litres   1250 ml   285 ml

E Answer these questions:

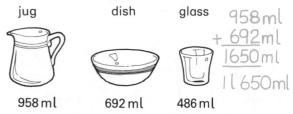

jug   dish   glass

958 ml   692 ml   486 ml

958 ml
+ 692 ml
1650 ml
1 l 650ml

☆ What is the total capacity of the jug and the dish?

1. What is the total capacity of the dish and the glass?

2. What is the total capacity of the jug and the glass?

3. What is the difference in capacity between the jug and the dish?

4. Is the capacity of the glass greater than $\frac{1}{2}$ litre or less than $\frac{1}{2}$ litre?

A Use multiplication to find how many blocks in these layers:

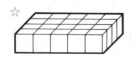 5 X 4 = 20

1 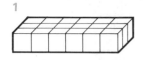 4

2 5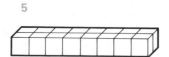

3 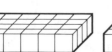 6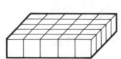

B Use multiplication to find how many blocks in these cuboids:

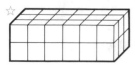

number of blocks in each layer	18
number of layers	x 2
number of blocks altogether	36

1 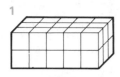 4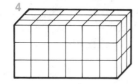

2 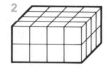 5

3 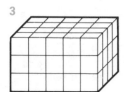 6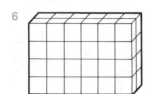

C Which of these shapes has the greater volume? Write **a** or **b**:

a 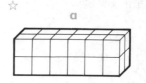 b 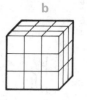 b

1 a 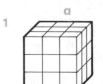 b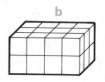

2 a 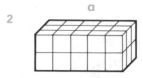 b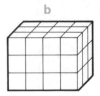

3 a 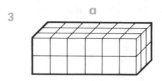 b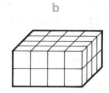

4 a 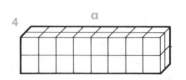 b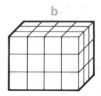

5 a 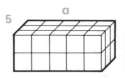 b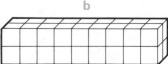

6 a 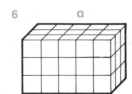 b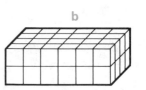

Volume

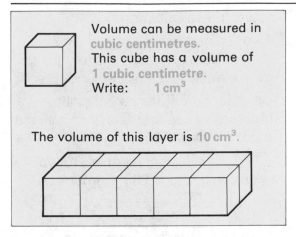

Volume can be measured in cubic centimetres.
This cube has a volume of 1 cubic centimetre.
Write: 1 cm³

The volume of this layer is 10 cm³.

The cuboids below have been made with centimetre cubes.
This cuboid has a volume of 16 cm³.

A The layers below have been made with centimetre cubes.
What is the **volume** of each layer?

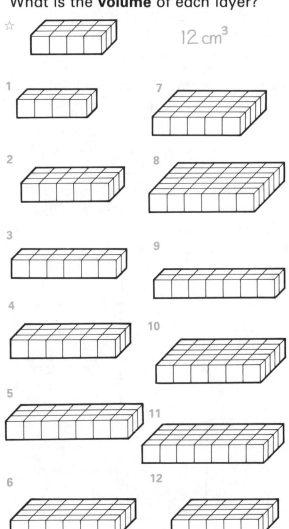

☆   12 cm³

1

2

3

4

5

6

7

8

9

10

11

12

B What is the **volume** of each of these cuboids?

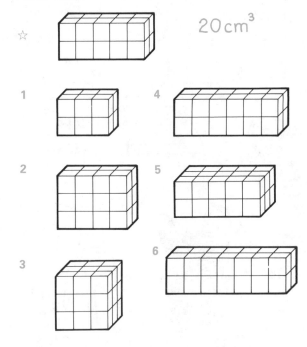

☆   20 cm³

1

2

3

4

5

6

C Use the cuboids in **B** to answer these questions:

1 Which cuboid has the greatest volume?

2 Which cuboid has the smallest volume?

3 Which two cuboids have the same volume?

4 Which cuboid has half the volume of cuboid 4?

A Copy and complete.
Show coins to pay each amount:

		£1	50p	20p	10p	5p	2p	1p
1	£1·54							
2	£2·85							
3	£4·79							
4	£3·99							

B Copy and complete:

	cost	money given	change
1	27p	50p	
2	52p	£1	
3	34p	£1	
4	£1·72	£5	

C

lamp
£18·27

basket
£8·94

coffee table £27·68

stool £11·23

1 What is the difference in price between a stool and a basket?

2 3 people share the cost of a basket. How much does each person pay?

3 Mr Holt gives £15 to pay for a stool. How much change does he receive?

4 What is the total cost of a coffee table, a lamp and a stool?

5 Mr Perch buys 4 stools. How much does he have to pay?

6 What is the difference in price between a basket and a coffee table?

D Answer these questions:

1 Two tables have lengths of 1·62 metres and 1·36 metres. How far do they stretch when placed end to end?

2 What is the difference in height between a tree that is 5·35 m tall and a bush that is 2·83 m high?

3 The distance between two airports is 289 kilometres.

If a plane makes 4 journeys of 289 kilometres, how far does it fly altogether?

4 A piece of rope 16·83 m long is cut into 3 equal pieces. What is the length of each piece?

E Write these capacities in **millilitres**:

1 $\frac{1}{2}$ l   4 0·2 l   7 $\frac{7}{10}$ l

2 $\frac{1}{10}$ l   5 0·8 l   8 2·2 l

3 $\frac{1}{5}$ l   6 1·1 l   9 2·6 l

F These cuboids have been made with centimetre cubes. What is the **volume** of each cuboid?

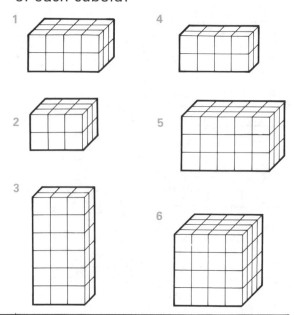

A How many metres in a kilometre?

Approximately how many times would you need to walk to your teacher's table and back in order to walk 1 kilometre?

Make a paper aeroplane and carry out three test flights.

Measure how far the plane travels in each flight.

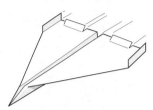

What is the longest distance your plane travelled to the nearest metre?

How many flights of this distance would your plane need to take in order to travel 1 km?

(You may use a calculator if this helps you.)

Your headteacher wants to keep fit by walking 1 kilometre around the school every day.

Plan a route for your headteacher so that after 500 metres there is water nearby and after 950 metres there is a place to sit down for a rest.

B You need a calculator.

Mr. Arthur Pint is cross. No-one seems to understand him.

He says that he weighs 9 stone and 7 pounds but he needs to know his weight in kilograms and grams.

He drinks $2\frac{1}{2}$ pints of liquid every day but he needs to know how many litres and millilitres he drinks.

He has a package to send through the post which is a cube measuring 1 foot by 1 foot by 1 foot. He has been asked if his package has a larger volume than a cube measuring $\frac{1}{2}$ metre by $\frac{1}{2}$ metre by $\frac{1}{2}$ metre.

Can you help Mr. Pint with his problems?

This information may help you:
1 stone = 14 pounds.
1 pound is approximately 454 grams.
1 pint is approximately 568 millilitres.
1 foot is approximately 30·5 centimetres.

Answer any questions you can. Leave those you cannot do.

Measure in centimetres the perimeter of each shape below:

1
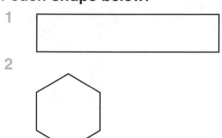

2

3 What is the perimeter of a rectangular pool with sides of 6 metres and 4 metres?

Write these lengths in metres and centimetres:

4 2·38 m   5 10·09 m

Two pieces of wood are joined end to end. What is the total length when:

6 Piece 1 measures 4 m 27 cm and Piece 2 measures 1 m 43 cm?

7 Piece 1 measures 6 m 30 cm and Piece 2 measures 306 cm?

Write these lengths in centimetres:

8 7·24 m

9 6·04 m

How much lower is a spider when:

10 it drops 85 cm and climbs back up 32 cm?

11 it drops 3 m 24 cm and climbs back up 1 m 62 cm?

12 What is the perimeter of a square lawn with sides of 10 m 25 cm?

Copy and complete:

13   6·8 3 m
    ×   7

14 5) 18·65 m

15 8) 93·84 m

Write these distances in kilometres and metres:

16 1864 m   17 7077 m

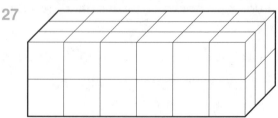

weight 246 g   weight 824 g   weight $\frac{1}{2}$ kg

capacity 260 mL capacity 1100 mL   capacity 2 l

18 What is the total weight of the glass and the jug?

19 What is the total weight of the jug and the saucepan?

20 What is the difference in weight between the saucepan and the glass?

21 What is the total capacity of the jug and the saucepan?

22 If a glass is filled from a full jug, how much water is left in the jug?

23 If a jug is filled from a full saucepan, how much water is left in the saucepan?

What are these weights in grams?

24 $\frac{1}{2}$ kg   25 3 kg   26 $\frac{1}{4}$ kg

This cuboid has been built with centimetre cubes. What is its volume?

27

28 The edge of a cube measures 3 cm. What is its volume?

Graphs

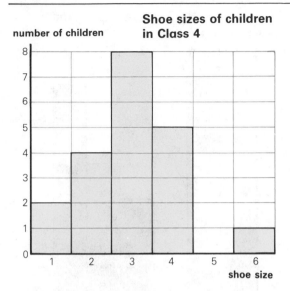

Shoe sizes of children in Class 4

A Use the **column graph** to answer these questions:

☆ How many children wear size 2 shoes? — 4

1 How many children wear size 3 shoes?

2 How many children wear size 6 shoes?

3 How many children wear size 5 shoes?

4 How many more children wear size 4 shoes than size 1 shoes?

5 How many fewer children wear size 6 shoes than size 3 shoes?

6 How many children are there in the class?

7 What is the total number of children wearing size 1, size 2 and size 3 shoes?

8 What is the total number of children wearing size 4, size 5 and size 6 shoes?

9 What fraction of the children in class 4 wear size 4 shoes?

10 What fraction of the children in class 4 wear size 2 shoes?

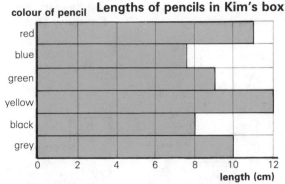

Lengths of pencils in Kim's box

B Use the graph to answer these questions:

☆ Which is the longest pencil? *yellow*

1 Which is the shortest pencil?

2 What is the length of the red pencil?

3 What is the difference in length between the grey pencil and the black pencil?

4 What is the difference in length between the red pencil and the black pencil?

5 If all the pencils were placed end to end, would they stretch further than 58 cm?

C This table shows the number of children absent from school during one week:

day	Mon	Tues	Weds	Thurs	Fri
number absent	10	18	14	7	20

Copy and complete this graph:

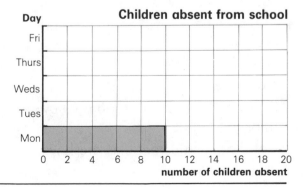

Children absent from school

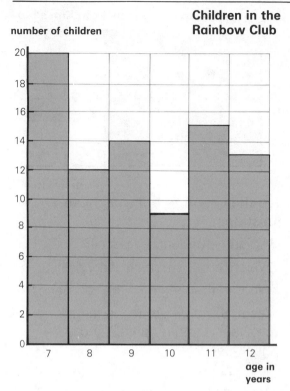

Children in the Rainbow Club

number of children

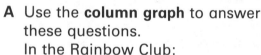

age in years

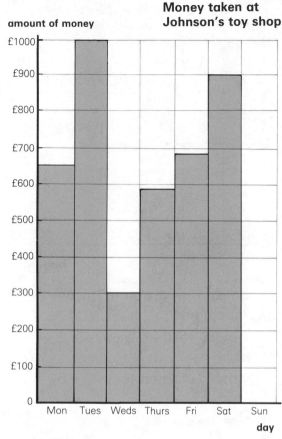

Money taken at Johnson's toy shop

amount of money

day

A Use the **column graph** to answer these questions.
In the Rainbow Club:

☆ how many children are under 9 years old?   *32*

1 how many children are over 10 years old?

2 how many more 7 year olds than 10 year olds are there?

3 how many children altogether are 8, 9 or 10?

4 how many fewer 12 year olds than 7 year olds are there?

5 are there more children under 9 or over 9?

6 how many children are there altogether?

7 if 57 go to the Summer Camp, how many do not go?

8 $\frac{1}{4}$ of the 7 and 8 year olds are boys, how many are girls?

B Use the **column graph** to answer these questions:

☆ On which day was no money taken?   *Sunday*

1 Why was no money taken on Sunday?

2 How much money was taken on Wednesday?

3 Why do you think less money was taken on Wednesday than on any other open days?

4 Was more money taken on Friday or on Monday?

5 On which day was the most money taken?

6 About how much money was taken on Monday?

7 About how much money was taken on Thursday?

Graphs

This graph is a **vertical line graph**.
It shows the amount of petrol in
a car's tank at different times.

amount of petrol (litres)

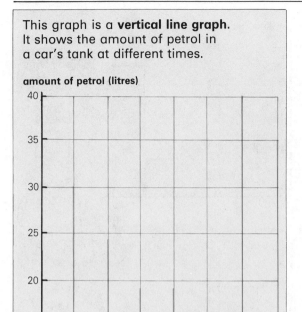

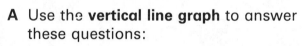

time

A Use the **vertical line graph** to answer
these questions:

☆ How much petrol was in the tank at
1.00 pm?   *30 litres*

1 How much petrol was in the tank at
6.00 pm?

2 How much petrol was in the tank at
7.00 pm?

3 How much more petrol was in the
tank at 6.00 pm than at 1.00 pm?

4 What do you think was happening to
the car between 3.00 pm and
4.00 pm?

5 Why is the reading at 6.00 pm
greater than at any other hour?

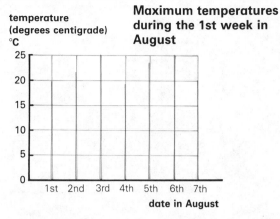

**temperature
(degrees centigrade)
°C**

**Maximum temperatures
during the 1st week in
August**

date in August

B Use the **vertical line graph** to answer
these questions:

☆ What was the highest temperature
during the week?   *25°c*

1 What was the highest temperature
on August 3rd?

2 What was the highest temperature
on August 5th?

3 Which day had a maximum
temperature 3 degrees higher than the
maximum temperature on August 4th?

This table shows the height of a
plane above the ground as it lands:

time	9.26	9.27	9.28	9.29	9.30	9.31
height	600 m	400 m	200 m	100 m	50 m	0 m

C Copy and complete this **vertical line
graph**:

**height above ground
(metres)**

**Height of plane
above the ground**

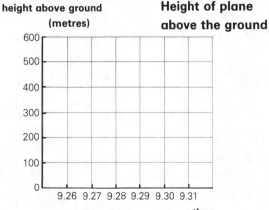

time

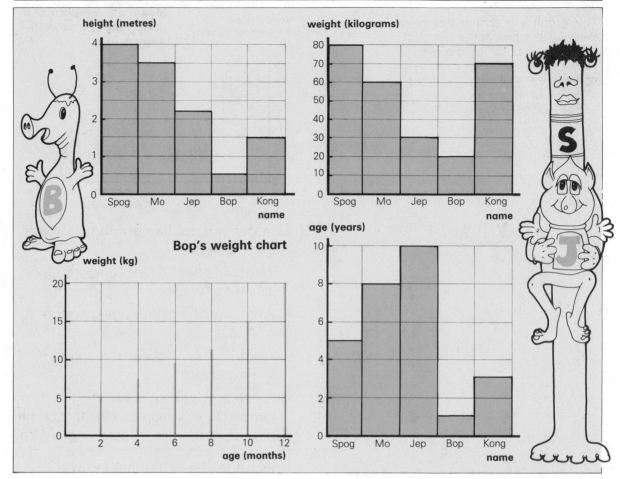

height (metres)

weight (kilograms)

Bop's weight chart

weight (kg)

age (months)

age (years)

A 1 Who is sitting on these scales?

SPACE SCALES
kilograms
70 kg

2 Who do you think has just received this card?

3 Which space people can walk through this door without bending?

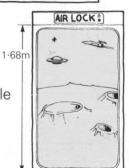

AIR LOCK
1·68m

B ☆ How much heavier is Spog than Jep?

50 kg

1 How much lighter than Mo is Bop?

2 How old was Bop when his weight was 15 kg?

3 What is the difference in height between Mo and Kong?

4 How much older than Kong is Jep?

5 A spaceship can carry no more than 250 kg. Can all 5 space people travel in the ship?

6 Three of the space people together weigh 130 kg. Who are they?

A This table shows the top teams in the Premier Division in October. The letters at the top of the table have these meanings: Pl = games played, Pts = points, GD = goal difference, W = won, D = drawn, L = lost, F = goals for, A = goals against.

		Pl	Pts	GD	W	D	L	F	A				Pl	Pts	GD	W	D	L	F	A
1	Newcastle	10	24	+10	8	0	2	20	10		5	Man Utd	10	19	+8	5	4	1	19	11
2	Arsenal	10	21	+11	6	3	1	19	8		6	Chelsea	10	16	+1	4	4	2	16	15
3	Wimbledon	10	21	+9	7	0	3	20	11		7	Aston Villa	10	15	+3	4	3	3	13	10
4	Liverpool	9	20	+11	6	2	1	18	7		8	Tottenham	10	14	+2	4	2	4	10	8

Copy and complete this column graph.

Draw 3 vertical line graphs to represent other information from the table.

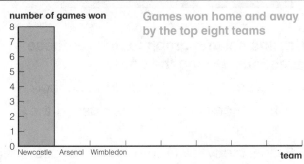

B Two straight lines cross at one point.

Three straight lines, all crossing each other, cross at 3 points.

The crossing points are called **points of intersection**.

How many points of intersection are there when 4 straight lines all cross each other?

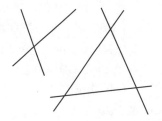

Copy this table ...

Carry out an investigation which will help you to fill in the missing information.

number of straight lines	2	3	4	5	6	7	8
number of points of intersection	1	3					28

Copy and complete this vertical line graph to show the information you have recorded in your table.

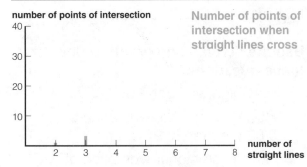

Answer any questions you can. Leave those you cannot do.

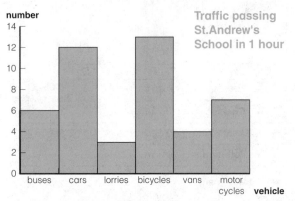

Traffic passing St.Andrew's School in 1 hour

Use the column graph to answer these questions. During the hour:

1 how many cars passed the school?

2 how many motor cycles passed the school?

3 how many fewer lorries than buses passed the school?

4 how many more bicycles than vans passed the school?

5 how many bicycles and motor cycles passed the school altogether?

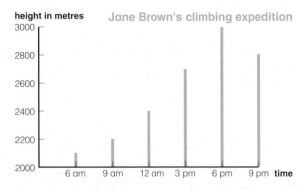

Jane Brown's climbing expedition

Use the vertical line graph to answer these questions:

6 How high was Jane at 3.00 pm?

7 How much higher was Jane at 9.00 pm than at 9.00 am?

8 How much higher was Jane at 6.00 pm than at 6.00 am?

9 If Jane rested between 12.00 am and 1.00 pm, how far did she climb in the 5 hours from 1.00 pm to 6.00 pm?

10 Jane started climbing at 6.00 am and finished climbing at 9.00 pm How much higher was she at the end of the day than at the start of the day?

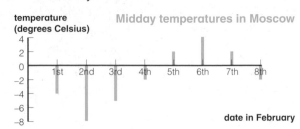

Midday temperatures in Moscow

Use the vertical line graph to answer these questions:

11 What was the midday temperature in Moscow on 3rd February?

12 What was the temperature at midday in Moscow on 7th February?

13 On 4th February, the temperature at 3 pm was 3 °C higher than the midday temperature. What was the temperature at 3 pm?

14 On 7th February the temperature dropped 8 °C in the 10 hours after midday. What was the temperature at 10.00 pm?

15 On 1st February the temperature at 2 pm was 2 °C lower than the midday temperature. What was the temperature at 2 pm?

16 On 8th February the temperature at 5 pm was 5 °C higher than the midday temperature. What was the temperature at 5 pm?

This graph shows the temperatures at 10.00 am in Aberdeen.

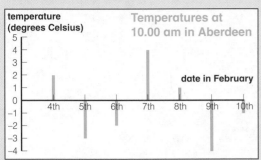

temperature (degrees Celsius)

Temperatures at 10.00 am in Aberdeen

date in February

On some days the temperature was below 0 °C. This is the temperature at which water will freeze.

On 6th January the temperature was –2°C or 'minus two degrees Celsius'.

A **What was the temperature in Aberdeen at 10.00 am on:**

☆ 8th January   1 °C

1 4th January?   3 5th January?

2 9th January?   4 10th January?

B **Write in words the temperature at 10.00 am on:**

☆ 9th January
  minus four degrees Celsius

1 7th January   3 8th January

2 4th January   4 5th January

C **What is the new temperature if:**

☆ the temperature is 3 °C and it falls by 4 °C?   –1 °C

1 the temperature is 2 °C and it falls by 3 °C?

2 the temperature is 0 °C and it falls by 2 °C?

3 the temperature is –4 °C and it rises by 7 °C?

This number line shows numbers less than 0. They are called negative numbers.

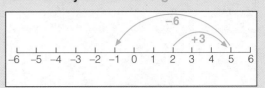

If you start with 2, add 3 and subtract 6 the answer is –1 (minus one).

D Write numbers for ✱'s.

☆ 3 – 5 = ✱   –2

1 6 – 8 = ✱

2 –1 + 4 – 3 = ✱

3 6 – 7 – 2 = ✱

4 8 + 2 – 12 = ✱

5 11 – 7 – 6 = ✱

E Write the answers to these questions:

☆ 5 + 4 – 11 = ✱   minus 2

1 6 – 9 = ✱

2 –7 + 4 = ✱

3 4 – 7 + 1 = ✱

4 2 + 8 – 13 = ✱

5 10 – 5 – 12 = ✱

F Use a calculator to answer these questions:

☆ 32 – 57 = ✱   –25

1 19 – 34 = ✱

2 23 + 42 – 77 = ✱

3 15 – 64 + 20 = ✱

4 2 – 39 + 17 = ✱

5 23 – 25 – 89 = ✱

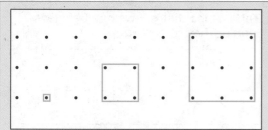

The first square above contains 1 dot.
The second square contains 4 dots.
The third square contains 9 dots.
When the pattern is continued, the
numbers of dots in each square are:

1   4   9   16   25   36
  +3   +5   +7   +9   +11   +13

This pattern can be continued by adding
on the odd numbers.

A In the pattern of squares above, how
many dots will you find in:

☆ the 6th square?   36

1 the 7th square?

2 the 9th square?

3 the 10th square?

4 the 12th square?

5 the 20th square?

B If this pattern of shapes is continued,
how many dots will you find in:

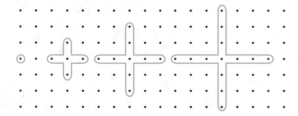

☆ the 5th shape?   17

1 the 6th shape?

2 the 7th shape?

3 the 10th shape?

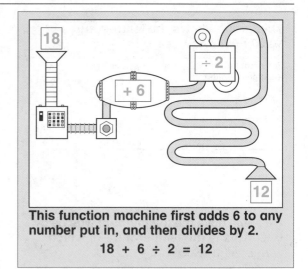

This function machine first adds 6 to any
number put in, and then divides by 2.

18 + 6 ÷ 2 = 12

C Write the missing signs for the
machines below.

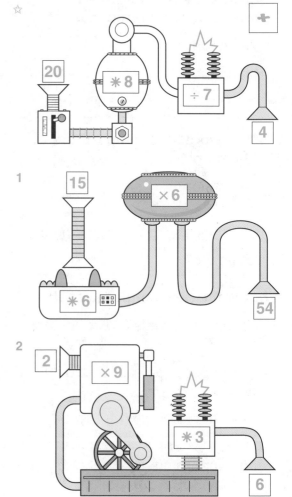

Number

linking operations, brackets 97

You can find the missing numbers in this addition by using subtraction:

```
  4 8
+ * *        71 − 48 = 23
  7 1
```

You can find the missing numbers in this division by using multiplication:

```
     6 3
9 ) * * *    63 × 9 = 567
```

By using signs and brackets, you can use the numbers above (3 4 5) to make the answer 35.

$$(3 + 4) \times 5 = 35$$

Always work out the part of the problem in brackets first.

You could use the same numbers to make the answer 27.

$$3 \times (4 + 5) = 27$$

A Use subtraction to find the missing numbers in these additions.

You may use a calculator.

☆
```
   * *
 + 2 5       88 − 25 = 63
   8 8
```

1
```
   5 9
 + * *
   9 1
```

4
```
   1 2 5
 + * * *
   4 8 2
```

2
```
   * *
 + 5 3
 1 3 0
```

5
```
   * * *
 + 3 7 7
   8 6 6
```

3
```
   6 9
 + * *
 1 2 7
```

6
```
   4 5 7
 + * * *
 1 2 3 4
```

B Use multiplication to find the missing numbers in these divisions.

You may use a calculator.

☆
```
      9 9
5 ) * * *    99 × 5 = 495
```

1
```
      6 8
7 ) * * *
```

4
```
      7 6
8 ) * * *
```

2
```
    2 1 3
4 ) * * *
```

5
```
    2 4 8
4 ) * * *
```

3
```
      7 5
9 ) * * *
```

6
```
    1 5 6 2
3 ) * * * *
```

C Write answers for the following:

☆ 2 + (2 × 4) = *   10

1 6 + (4 × 3) = *

2 (9 − 5) × 6 = *

3 (3 × 6) − 12 = *

4 100 + (60 + 40) = *

5 (56 ÷ 7) × 8 = *

6 (90 ÷ 10) + 19 = *

7 16 + (8 × 11) = *

8 3 × (27 + 27) = *

D Use signs and brackets with the numbers below to make the answers given:

☆ 3   3   4 = 13

(3 × 3) + 4 = 13

1 6   4   8 = 38

2 4   9   2 = 34

3 5   7   3 = 36

4 9   5   7 = 38

5 8   10   22 = 102

6 100   10   9 = 90

7 64   8   9 = 72

8 12   4   12 = 60

A For each of the following write certain, impossible or might happen.

☆ You will have a drink in the next two weeks.   certain

1 Tomorrow you will swim 1000 km.

2 Somewhere in the world a bird will fly today.

3 The next person who walks through your classroom door will wear shoes larger than yours.

B Say if each of the following events is likely, unlikely, certain or impossible.

☆ If you roll a dice numbered 1 to 6 you will roll a number greater than 1.   likely

1 If you spin 4 coins all 4 coins will land as heads.

2 The first day next year will be February 1st.

3 The next time you roll a dice you will score a 6.

C What is the chance of drawing an orange counter from these bags? Write very likely, likely, even chance, unlikely or very unlikely.

☆    very unlikely

1 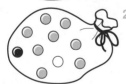   2

> You can show the chance of something happening by using a probability fraction.
> If there are 4 counters in a bag and 3 are red, the chance of drawing a red counter is 3 in 4. The probability fraction is $\frac{3}{4}$
> If you spin 2 coins there are 4 possible results:
>
>
>
> The chances of spinning a head and a tail is 2 in 4 or $\frac{1}{2}$

D Work out the probability fraction for each of the following:

☆   Rolling a 5 on a dice numbered 1 to 6. $\frac{1}{6}$

1   Drawing a black counter from a bag containing 3 black counters and 1 orange counter.

2 Finding a diamond at the top of a pack of cards after they have been shuffled.

3 Rolling a 1 or a 2 on a dice numbered 1 to 6.

4 Scoring 1 or 10 on a spinner numbered 1 to 10.

5  Choosing the letter 'E' from a set of tiles showing each of the letters of the alphabet.

6  Finding 2 heads when 2 coins are spun together.

The chance of something happening can also be shown as a decimal.

The chance of a spinning coin landing as a tail is $\frac{1}{2}$ or 0·5.

The chance of the top card in a pack of cards being a club is $\frac{1}{4}$ or 0·25.

If something is impossible the chance of it happening is 0.

If something is certain the chance of it happening is $\frac{1}{1}$ or 1.

The chance of something happening can be shown on a probability scale.

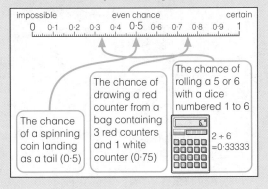

The chance of a spinning coin landing as a tail (0·5)

The chance of drawing a red counter from a bag containing 3 red counters and 1 white counter (0·75)

The chance of rolling a 5 or 6 with a dice numbered 1 to 6

$2 \div 6 = 0.33333$

A Show as a decimal the probability of each of these things happening:

☆ Scoring an even number with a spinner numbered 1 to 10. 0·5

1  Finding 1 head and 1 tail when 2 coins are spun together.

2 Drawing an orange counter from a bag containing 4 orange counters and 6 black counters.

3 The next hexagon you draw having 6 sides.

4 The next person who visits your class being a Martian.

5 Spinning a number less than 5 with a spinner numbered 1 to 10.

6 Scoring a total of 13 when two dice numbered 1 to 6 are rolled.

B Draw your own probability scale like the one above.

Show with arrows on your scale the chance of these events happening:

☆ Scoring a '3' with a spinner numbered 1 to 10.   0·3

1 Having a red card on the top of a pack after the pack has been shuffled.

2 Finding 2 tails when 2 coins are spun together.

3 Spinning an odd number with a spinner numbered 1 to 10.

4 Scoring a total of '1' when 2 dice are rolled.

5  Having a heart, diamond or spade on the top of a pack after the cards have been shuffled.

6 Rolling a 4, 5 or 6 with a dice numbered 1 to 6.

A

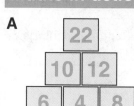

In this brick wall, each brick shows the total of the two bricks below.

The bottom row of bricks can be arranged in 6 different ways.

What difference does the order of bricks in the bottom row make to the total in the top brick?

Repeat this investigation with 2 more sets of 3 numbers.

Each time you make a highest total, what do you notice about the number in the middle brick on the bottom row?

Investigate what happens when you make a bottom row of 4 bricks.

How would you arrange the numbers to give the highest total in the top brick?

B Marco has put 10 counters in a bag. He takes one out, records the colour and returns the counter to the bag. He repeats this 50 times. This table shows his results:

colour of counter	red	green	blue	white
number of times chosen	24	11	4	11

Guess how many counters of each colour are in the bag. Explain your answer.

From this investigation, Marco can say that the probability of drawing a red counter is approximately 24 out of 50 or 0·48. (24 ÷ 50 = 0·48)

He has shown this on a probability scale.

$$0 \quad 0·1 \quad 0·2 \quad 0·3 \quad 0·4 \quad 0·5 \quad 0·6 \quad 0·7 \quad 0·8 \quad 0·9 \quad 1$$

For each of the following investigations, draw a red arrow on a probability scale to show what you think the result might be.

Carry out 50 trials and draw a black arrow on the probability scale to show your result.

INVESTIGATION 1. Finding 3 heads when you spin three coins

INVESTIGATION 2. Scoring a total of 7 when you roll 2 dice

INVESTIGATION 3. Finding an ace on the top of a pack after you have shuffled the cards

Answer any questions you can. Leave those you cannot do.

What is the missing number in each pattern?

1 80   83   86   89   92   95   98   ✱

2 65   61   ✱   53   49   45

3 800   400   200   100   ✱   25

4 1   4   9   16   ✱   36

5 900   925   950   975   1000   ✱

What will be the tenth number in each of these patterns?

6 1   6   11   16   21   26   ....

7 2   3   5   6   8   9   ....

8 1024   512   256   128   64   32   ....

9 1   1   2   3   5   8   ....

10 1   3   6   10   15   21   ....

Write the number missing from this function machine:

11
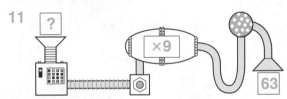

Write the signs missing from this function machine:

12
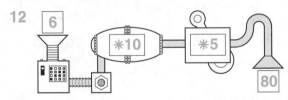

Write down the value of each letter:

13 32 × 10 = 64 × **Y**

14 $\frac{20}{4} = \frac{40}{K}$

15 15 + **L** = 29

16 3**Y** − 8 = **Y** + 14

Write answers for the following:

17 6 − 7 = ✱

18 5 − 10 = ✱

19 4 + 2 − 10 = ✱

20 1 − 9 + 6 = ✱

21 2 − 11 + 12 = ✱

Write answers for the following:

22 5 + (3 × 2) = ✱

23 (4 × 5) − 7 = ✱

24 32 − (35 ÷ 7) = ✱

25 (64 ÷ 8) × 4 = ✱

For each of the following events, say if they are certain, impossible or might happen:

26 Someone in the world will see the sun tomorrow.

27 When you spin 2 coins neither will land as a tail.

28 If you add together 2 odd numbers the total will be an odd number.

29 You will sleep during the next week.

Work out the probability fraction for each of the following:

30 Rolling an even number with a dice numbered 1 to 6.

31 Spinning a number less than 5 with a spinner numbered 1 to 10.

32 Choosing a red counter from a bag containing 4 red counters, 2 blue counters and 4 yellow counters.

Which arrow on the probability scale best shows the chance of this event happening, A, B or C?

33 Choosing a black counter from a bag containing 5 black counters and 20 red counters.

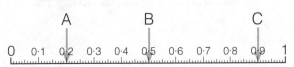

Where are you going Harry?

You need 21 counters.
Cover squares with answers **greater than 50**, to find who
Harry is visiting.

Harry Hedgehog	10×6	2)686	12×5	32+26	9)477	76−24	5)245
6×8	3)138	24+25	68−30	6×6	102−64	6×9	4)96
4)184	100−55	4×9	22+25	7)434	119+50	10+42	11×4
5×10	117−70	6)426	44+17	16+35	5×9	102−81	7)196
32+16	6)228	100−45	7×5	36+11	8)376	99−49	Molly Mole
Fred Fox	72−28	7×9	143−92	8×7	200−142	5)235	25+25
9×5	7+39	16+25	7)343	126−78	6)522	101−52	6×7
Antony Ant	3)132	7×7	Wally Worm	9)702	8×8	29+12	Roberto Rabbit

Mixed problems

A Work out the answers to these problems:

☆ A gardener has 1276 apple trees and 2185 plum trees. How many trees does he have altogether?

$$\begin{array}{r} 1276 \\ +2185 \\ \hline 3461 \end{array}$$

1 Alan Upside climbed 2185 metres on Saturday and 1425 metres on Sunday. How far did he climb during the weekend?

2 Jenny Speed is saving for a new car. If the car costs £6235 and she has saved £2444, how much more does she need?

3 A train journey takes $3\frac{1}{4}$ hours. If the journey ends at 8.10 pm at what time did it start?

4 If glasses hold 86 millilitres, what is the total capacity of 6 glasses?

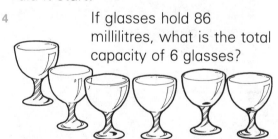

5 Mrs Bloom has 272 flowers. How many bunches of 8 flowers can she make?

6 9 people hire a boat at a cost of £747. If they share the cost equally, how much does each person pay?

B Work out the answers to these:

☆ What is the product of 26 and 5?

$$\begin{array}{r} 26 \\ \times\ 5 \\ \hline 130 \end{array}$$

1 How many pencils are left over when 474 pencils are packed in tens?

2 Mrs Box has a rectangular dining-room. The length of the room is 7 m and the width of the room is 4 m. What is the area of the floor?

3 If Bob eats $\frac{2}{5}$ of a cake and Jane eats $\frac{1}{10}$ of the cake, what fraction of the cake is left?

4 What is the product of 2·7 and 8?

5 There are 36 people on a bus. If one-third of the people get off, how many people are left on the bus?

6 14·6 kg of seeds are taken from a sack holding 32·8 kg of seeds. What weight of seeds is left?

7 The length of a swimming pool is 24·7 m. Pat swims 5 lengths. How far does she swim?

8 If you have £16·91 and buy a hamster for £4·95, how much money do you have left?

A 1 Write in figures two thousand three hundred and sixty-two.

2 $96 - 52 = $ *

3 $9 \times 7 = $ *

4 How many books is $\frac{1}{8}$ of 32 books?

5 How many degrees make 2 right angles?

6 How many days in November?

7 Write $\frac{71}{100}$ as a decimal.

8 What is the volume of a cube with sides of 2 cm?

B 1 $160 + 80 = $ *

2 $64 \div 8 = $ *

3 What is the product of 12 and 6?

4 How many 100 g weights balance $\frac{1}{2}$ kg?

5 How many sides of an equilateral triangle are equal in length?

6 What time will it be 4 hours after 6.00 am?

7 $\frac{2}{3} = \frac{*}{6}$

8 Would you measure the capacity of an egg cup in litres, grams, millimetres or millilitres?

C 1 $100 - 65 = $ *

2 Write $\frac{7}{10}$ as a decimal.

3 $6 \times 8 = $ *

4 The length of a rectangle is 7 cm. The breadth is 5 cm. What is the area of the rectangle?

5 If you are facing North and turn through 3 right angles clockwise, which direction will you be facing?

6 $\frac{1}{3} + \frac{1}{6} = \frac{*}{6}$

7 What is the probability fraction for spinning a tail when you spin a coin?

8 $57{\cdot}0 \div 10 = $ *

D 1 $59 + 49 = $ *

2 How much change will you receive if you give £5 to pay for a snack costing £2.73?

3 $90 \div $ * $= 9$

4 If 26th March is a Wednesday, what day is 7th April?

5 Is an angle of 100° acute or obtuse?

6 $(500 - 50) \times 10 = $ *

7 What time will it be $1\frac{1}{2}$ hours after 7.30 pm?

8 How many grams in $2\frac{1}{2}$ kg?

E 1 Write 0·8 as a fraction.

2 $64 + $ * $= 101$

3 How many fish is $\frac{3}{10}$ of 60 fish?

4 A rectangular carpet measures 8 m by 7 m. What is its area?

5 How many lines of symmetry has an equilateral triangle?

6 What is the cost of 4 yoghurts costing 53p each?

7 $289 + 982 = 1271$
$1271 - 982 = $ *

8 $2.6 \times 10 = $ *

F 1 $109 - 47 = $ *

2 * $\div 9 = 7$

3 $7 \times 7 = $ *

4 What time will it be 10 minutes after 6.55 pm?

5 If the radius of a circle is 5 cm, what is the length of its diameter?

6 26·3 kg of flour is taken from a sack containing 40 kg. How much flour is left in the sack?

7 Write as a decimal 26 hundredths.

8 $26 + 62 + $ * $= 111$

A
1 Write in figures nine thousand and thirteen.
2 What are the factors of 8?
3 Jack is 1 m 68 cm tall. Jill is 1·8 m tall. How much taller is Jill than Jack?
4 How many degrees make $\frac{1}{2}$ a right angle?
5 What time will it be $\frac{1}{4}$ hour after 5.05 am?
6 What is the area of a rectangular lawn with a length of 100 m and a breadth of 28 m?
7 What is the volume of a cube with sides of 5 cm?

B
1 $92 - ✱ = 59$
2 How many bunches of 8 flowers can be made with 88 flowers?
3 $6 × 6 = ✱$
4 One side of a square measures 9 m. What is its area?
5 How many sides of a scalene triangle are equal in length?
6 How many days in February if it is a leap year?
7 A cake weighs 3·4 kg. What is the weight of $\frac{1}{2}$ of the cake?

C
1 $2100 - 1200 = ✱$
2 A car can travel 9·48 km using 1 litre of petrol. How far can it travel using 10 litres of petrol?
3 $650 ÷ 10 = ✱$
4 $\frac{4}{5} = \frac{8}{✱}$
5 How many sides in an isosceles triangle are equal in length?
6 How many 50 g weights balance $\frac{1}{2}$ kg?
7 $(3 + 8) × 4 = ✱$

D
1 $101 - ✱ = 53$
2 $9 × 98 = ✱$
3 What is the probability fraction for rolling a '5' with a dice numbered 1 to 6?
4 What time is 16 minutes earlier than 8.21 pm?
5 How many right angles in a square?
6 How much is $\frac{3}{4}$ of £84?
7 What is 3628 metres in kilometres and metres?
8 A cuboid has sides of 2 cm, 4 cm and 6 cm. What is its volume?

E
1 $3100 ÷ 10 = ✱$
2 What is the product of 32 and 10?
3 Write in figures nine thousand and ninety-nine.
4 Which fraction is smaller, $\frac{7}{10}$ or $\frac{4}{5}$?
5 Is an angle of 67° acute or obtuse?
6 What is the area of a square with sides of 12 m?
7 Write in millilitres 2·3 l.
8 How many 50 g weights balance $\frac{1}{4}$ kg?

F
1 $1000 - 250 = ✱$
2 Write $4\frac{7}{10}$ as a decimal.
3 $6 × ✱ = 54$
4 $\frac{1}{8} + \frac{3}{4} = \frac{✱}{8}$
5 What time is 23 minutes earlier than 9.19 pm?
6 $1200 + 316 = ✱$
7 A cuboid has sides of 4 cm, 5 cm and 6 cm. What is its volume?
8 What is the value of the 6 in the number 8602?

A 1 What is the difference in weight between 2 parcels weighing 0·75 kg and 900 g?

2 1511 + 111 = ✳

3 How many centimetres in 5·91 metres?

4 What are the factors of 21?

5 How many equal sides has a rhombus?

6 Which fraction is larger, $\frac{3}{4}$ or $\frac{5}{8}$?

7 How many people can be given a £10 prize from £4000?

B 1 151 − 39 = ✳

2 11 × ✳ = 99

3 Write 2695 ml in litres and millilitres.

4 A train journey takes $1\frac{3}{4}$ hours. If the train arrives at 2.52 pm, at what time did the journey start?

5 How many degrees make a complete turn?

6 Jenny had £48. She spent $\frac{5}{8}$ of this. How much had she left?

7 What is the total length of wood when 4 pieces of wood each measuring 1·09 m are joined end to end?

C 1 How many tenths make 7 units?

2 How many hundreds are there in 1400?

3 ✳ ÷ 10 = 100

4 How many degrees make 3 right angles?

5 $\frac{2}{5}$ + $\frac{3}{10}$ = $\frac{✳}{10}$

6 Which is the longer distance, 3068 m or three kilometres one hundred metres?

7 Use signs and brackets to make this answer correct: 6 9 3 = 45.

D 1 What is the difference in cost between 2 vans costing £5500 and £2150?

2 How many days in a leap year?

3 Phil Tired completes a marathon in 4 hours 28 minutes. If he started running at 2.20 pm at what time did he finish?

4 How many lines of symmetry has a rectangle?

5 ✳ × 10 = 190

6 5·3 − 2·8 = ✳

E 1 3150 + ✳ = 5000

2 6 + (9 × 3) = ✳

3 Six cinema tickets cost £25.20. What is the cost of each ticket?

4 If you are facing West and turn through 1 right angle clockwise, which direction will you be facing?

5 A full barrel holds 72 litres. If $\frac{4}{9}$ of the water is used, how many litres are left?

6 If 10th June is a Friday, what day is 1st July?

F 1 Mr. Gotalot has £10 000. If he spends £2950, how much has he left?

2 How many hundreds are there in 6200?

3 3·7 + 2·6 = ✳

4 Circle A has a radius of 3 cm. Circle B has a diameter of 5 cm. Which circle has the longer circumference?

5 What is the perimeter of a rectangle which has a length of 16 cm and a breadth of 15 cm?

6 Which is the greater capacity, 0·6 l or 609 ml?